The Truman and Eisenhower Years
1945 - 1960

A Selective Bibliography

by
Margaret L. Stapleton

The Scarecrow Press, Inc.
Metuchen, N.J.   1973

Library of Congress Cataloging in Publication Data

Stapleton, Margaret L
    The Truman and Eisenhower years: 1945-1960.

    Bibliography: p.
    1. United States--History--1945-   --Bibliography.
2. Truman, Harry S., Pres. U. S., 1884-1972--Bibliog-
raphy.   3. Eisenhower, Dwight David, Pres. U. S.,
1890-1969--Bibliography.   I. Title.
Z1245.S7   016.973918   73-1791
ISBN 0-8108-0601-0

FOREWORD

This bibliography offers a selection of over 1, 600 works published through June, 1972. It covers United States political, economic and social history of the administrations of Harry S Truman and Dwight D. Eisenhower. Its subject arrangement has required the occasional listing of works under more than one subject. It is assumed that a student wishing references on particular phases of history will also consult the general works.

The intense concern of the time with foreign affairs and national security is reflected by the large number of entries in these fields.

Only second in intensity is the interest in loyalty, civil liberties and civil rights. Social and intellectual history is covered less fully. No attempt has been made to survey the history of literature or art, or to cover the dissertation field.

To what extent should a historical bibliography be limited to works of recognized scholarship? I have assumed that the temper of the times can best be understood by examining also the popular writings, including some of the least scholarly. In making this more inclusive sweep the choice is in line with the external school of intellectual history of which Merle Curti is an exponent.

It is hoped that the work will prove useful to upper division and graduate students, to their teachers and to librarians.

I must express my thanks to Professor Robert E. Burke of the History Department of the University of Washington for his generous and time-consuming counsel in the preparation of this work.

M. S.

CONTENTS

vii

I. GENERAL

A. BIBLIOGRAPHICAL GUIDES

1. American Historical Association. Writings on American History, 1948-1959, Washington: Government Printing Office, 1952-1969. 12 vols.

2. American History Periodical Index, vol. 1-11, January, 1958-October, 1968.

3. Becker, Harold K. and Felkenes, George T. Law Enforcement: A Selected Bibliography. Metuchen, N. J.: Scarecrow Press, 1968.

4. Blanchard, Carroll Henry. Korean War Bibliography and Maps of Korea. Albany: Korean Conflict Research Foundation, 1964.

5. Burr, Nelson R. A Critical Bibliography of Religion in America. Princeton: Princeton University Press, 1961. 2 vols. (Religion in American Life, Vol. IV).

6. Corker, Charles. Bibliography on the Communist Problem in the United States. New York: Fund for the Republic, 1955. Compiled under the direction of Charles Corker.

7. Handlin, Oscar, and others. Harvard Guide to American History. Cambridge: The Belknap Press of Harvard University Press, 1954.

8. Harvard University. Library. American History: Classification Schedule. Cambridge: Distributed by Harvard University Press for the Harvard University Library, 1967. 5 vols.

9. Kirkendall, Richard S., ed. The Truman Period As a Research Field. Columbia: University of Missouri Press, 1967. Papers from a conference held in the Truman Library in April 1966.

1

10.   Miller, Elizabeth W. and Fisher, Mary L.   The Negro
       in America: A Bibliography.   2d ed. rev. and enl.
Cambridge: Harvard University Press, 1970.   First published 1966.

11.   Neufeld, Maurice F.   A Representative Bibliography
       of American Labor History.   Ithaca: Cornell Univer-
sity Press, 1964.

12.   Paulsen, David Frederick.   Natural Resources in the
       Government Process: A Bibliography.   Tucson: Uni-
versity of Arizona Press, 1970.

13.   Plischke, Elmer.   American Foreign Relations: A
       Bibliography of Official Sources.   College Park: Uni-
versity of Maryland, 1955.

14.   Roberts, Henry L. and others.   Foreign Affairs Bib-
       liography: A Selected and Annotated List of Books on
International Relations, 1942-1952.   New York: Published
for the Council on Foreign Relations by Harper, 1955.

15.   _____.   Foreign Affairs Bibliography: A Selected
       and Annotated List of Books on International Relations,
1952-1962.   New York: Published for the Council on
Foreign Relations by R. R. Bowker, 1960.

16.   Seidman, Joel Isaac.   Communism in the United
       States: A Bibliography.   Ithaca: Cornell University
Press, 1969.   A revision of Bibliography on the Communist
Problem in the United States, by Charles Corker.

17.   Stroud, Gene S. and Donahue, Gilbert E.   Labor
       History in the United States: A General Bibliography.
Urbana: Institute of Labor and Industrial Relations, 1961.
(Bibliographic Contributions No. 6)

18.   Trask, David F., Meyer, Michael C., and Trask,
       Roger R.   A Bibliography of United States-Latin
American Relations Since 1810: A Selected List of Eleven
Thousand Published References.   Lincoln: University of
Nebraska Press, 1968.

                  B.   GENERAL SURVEYS

19.   Agar, Herbert.   The Price of Power: America Since

1945. Chicago: University of Chicago Press, 1957. English title: The Unquiet Years: U.S.A. 1945-1955.

20. Commager, Henry S., ed. Documents of American History. 8th ed. New York: Appleton-Century-Crofts, 1968. Vol. II, Since 1898.

21. Goldman, Eric F. The Crucial Decade--and After: America, 1945-1960. New York: Vintage Books, 1960. Supersedes The Crucial Decade. New York: Knopf, 1956.

22. Morris, Richard B., ed. Encyclopedia of American History. Enl. and updated ed. New York: Harper & Row, 1970.

23. Mowry, George E. The Urban Nation, 1920-1960. New York: Hill and Wang, 1965. (The Making of America).

24. Murrow, Edward R. In Search of Light: The Broadcasts of Edward R. Murrow, 1938-1961. New York: Knopf, 1967.

25. Tugwell, Rexford G. Off Course: From Truman to Nixon. New York: Praeger, 1971.

II. GOVERNMENT AND POLITICS

A. GENERAL

26. American Political Science Association. Committee
on Political Parties. Toward a More Responsible
Two-Party System: A Report. New York: Rinehart, 1950.

27. Bowles, Chester. American Politics in a Revolutionary
World. Cambridge: Harvard University Press, 1956.
(Godkin Lectures)

28. _____. The Coming Political Breakthrough. New
York: Harper, 1959.

29. _____. Promises to Keep: My Years in Public
Life. New York: Harper & Row, 1971.

30. Brock, Clifton. Americans for Democratic Action:
Its Role in National Politics. Washington: Public
Affairs Press, 1962.

31. Brown, Stuart Gerry. Conscience in Politics: Adlai
E. Stevenson in the 1950's. Syracuse: Syracuse
University Press, 1962.

32. Brzezinski, Zbigniew K. and Huntington, Samuel P.
Political Power: USA/USSR. New York: Viking
Press, 1964

33. Burns, James MacGregor. The Deadlock of Democracy:
Four Party Politics in America. Englewood Cliffs,
N. J.: Prentice-Hall, 1963.

34. Caridi, Ronald J. The Korean War and American
Politics: The Republican Party As a Case Study.
Philadelphia: University of Pennsylvania Press, 1969.

35. Cater, Douglass. Power in Washington: A Critical
Look at Today's Struggle to Govern in the Nation's
Capital. New York: Random House, 1964.

4

36. Cheever, Daniel S. and Haviland, H. Field. American
     Foreign Policy and the Separation of Powers. Cam-
bridge: Harvard University Press, 1952.

37. Congressional Quarterly Service, Washington, D. C.
     Politics in America, 1945-1966. 2d ed. Washington:
Congressional Quarterly Service, 1967.

38. Dalfiume, Richard M. , ed. American Politics Since
     1945. Chicago: Quadrangle Books, 1969. (A New
York Times Book).

39. Deakin, James. The Lobbyists. Washington: Public
     Affairs Press, 1966.

40. Dorsett, Lyle W. The Pendergast Machine. New
     York: Oxford University Press, 1968.

41. Evans, Rowland and Novak, Robert. Lyndon B. John-
     son: The Exercise of Power. New York: The New
American Library, 1966.

42. Flynn, John T. The Decline of the American Republic
     and How to Rebuild It. New York: Devin-Adair, 1955.

43. Friendly, Henry J. The Federal Administrative
     Agencies: The Need for Better Definition of Standards.
Cambridge: Harvard University Press, 1962.

44. Fuchs, Lawrence H. The Political Behavior of Ameri-
     can Jews. Glencoe: Free Press, 1956.

45. Gervasi, Frank Henry. Big Government: The Mean-
     ing and Purpose of the Hoover Commission Report.
New York: Whittlesey House, 1949.

46. Goldwater, Barry. The Conscience of a Conservative.
     Shepherdsville, Ky. , Victor Publishing Company, 1960.

47. Harris, Joseph P. , "The Senatorial Rejection of Le-
     land Olds: A Case Study. " [1949] American Political
Science Review, XLV, (September, 1951), 674-692.

48. Harris, Seymour Edwin. The Economics of the Po-
     litical Parties: With Special Attention to Presidents
Eisenhower and Kennedy. New York: Macmillan, 1962.

49. Hoover, Herbert Clark. Addresses upon the American
     Road, 1945-1948. New York: Van Nostrand, 1949.

50. _____. Addresses upon the American Road, 1948-
     1950. Stanford: Stanford University Press, 1951.

51. Kelley, Stanley. Professional Public Relations and
     Political Power. Baltimore: Johns Hopkins Press,
     1956.

52. Lane, Robert E. The Regulation of Businessmen:
     Social Conditions of Government Economic Control.
New Haven: Yale University Press, 1954. (Originally published as Yale Studies in Political Science, v. 1)

53. Larson, Arthur. A Republican Looks at His Party.
     New York: Harper, 1956.

54. Lubell, Samuel. The Future of American Politics.
     3rd ed. rev. New York: Harper & Row, 1965.
First published 1952.

55. _____. The Revolt of the Moderates. New York:
     Harper, 1956.

56. Mann, Dean E. and Doig, Jameson W. The Assistant
     Secretaries: Problems and Processes of Appointment.
Washington: Brookings Institution, 1965.

57. Martin, Joseph W. and Donovan, R. J. My First
     Fifty Years in Politics. New York: McGraw-Hill,
     1960. As told to Robert J. Donovan.

58. Mayhew, David R. Party Loyalty among Congressmen:
     The Difference between Democrats and Republicans,
     1947-1962. Cambridge: Harvard University Press, 1966.

59. Mazo, Earl and Hess, Stephen. Nixon: A Political
     Portrait. New York: Harper & Row, 1968. An up-
dating of Richard Nixon (1959). ("A new book rather than
a revised edition. ")

60. _____. Richard Nixon: A Political and Personal
     Portrait. New York: Harper, 1959.

61. Milligan, Maurice M. Missouri Waltz: The Inside
     Story of the Pendergast Machine by the Man Who

Smashed It. New York: Scribner's, 1948.

62. Mooney, Booth. The Politicians: 1945-1960. Phila-
     delphia: Lippincott, 1970.

63. Morgenthau, Hans J. The Purpose of American
     Politics. New York: Knopf, 1960.

64. Nash, Bradley D. and Lynde, Cornelius. A Hook in
     Leviathan: A Critical Interpretation of the Hoover Com-
mission Report. New York: Macmillan, 1950.

65. Reichley, James, Behrens, Earl, and others. States
     in Crisis: Politics in Ten American States, 1950-1962.
Chapel Hill: University of North Carolina Press, 1964.

66. Roper, Elmo. You and Your Leaders: Their Actions
     and Your Reactions, 1936-1956. New York: Morrow,
1957.

67. Rose, Arnold M. The Power Structure: Political Pro-
     cess in American Society. New York: Oxford Uni-
versity Press, 1967.

68. Sawyer, Charles. Concerns of a Conservative Demo-
     crat. Carbondale, Southern Illinois University Press,
1968. Autobiography of Truman's Secretary of Commerce.

69. Schaffer, Alan. Vito Marcantonio, Radical in Congress.
     Syracuse: Syracuse University Press, 1966.

70. Schapsmeier, Edgar L. and Schapsmeier, Frederick
     H. Prophet in Politics: Henry A. Wallace and the
War Years, 1940-1965. Ames: Iowa State University
Press, 1970.

71. Scheele, Henry Z. Charlie Halleck: A Political Biog-
     raphy. New York: Exposition Press, 1966.

72. Schmidt, Karl M. Henry A. Wallace, Quixotic Cru-
     sader. Syracuse: Syracuse University Press, 1960.

73. Shadegg, Stephen C. Barry Goldwater: Freedom Is
     His Flight Plan. New York: Fleet Publishing Cor-
poration, 1962.

74. Smith, Arthur Robert. The Tiger in the Senate: The

    Biography of Wayne Morse.   Garden City: Doubleday,
1962.

75.   Somers, Herman Miles, "The Federal Bureaucracy
      and the Change of Administration," _American Political_
Science Review, XLVIII (March, 1954), 131-151.

76.   Stromer, Marvin E.   _The Making of a Political Leader:_
      Kenneth S. Wherry and the United States Senate.   Lin-
coln: University of Nebraska Press, 1969.

77.   Truman, David B.   _The Governmental Process: Poli-_
      tical Interests and Public Opinion.   New York: Knopf,
1951.

78.   U. S. Commission on Organization of the Executive
      Branch of the Government.   _The Hoover Commission_
Report on Organization of the Executive Branch of the
Government.   New York: McGraw-Hill, 1949.

79.   U. S. Office of Contract Settlement.   _A History of War_
      Contract Terminations and Settlements.   Washington:
Author, 1947.

80.   Westin, Alan F. , ed.   _The Uses of Power: 7 Cases in_
      American Politics.   New York: Harcourt, Brace and
World, 1962.

81.   White, William S.   _The Professional: Lyndon B._
      Johnson.   Boston: Houghton Mifflin, 1964.

82.   _____.   _The Responsibles_.   New York: Harper &
      Row, 1972.

83.   _____.   _The Taft Story_.   New York: Harper &
      Row, 1954.

84.   Wills, Garry.   _Nixon Agonistes: The Crisis of the_
      Self-Made Man.   Boston: Houghton Mifflin, 1970.

B.   THE PRESIDENCY

85.   Allen, George E.   _Presidents Who Have Known Me_.
      New York: Simon & Schuster, 1960.   First pub. 1950.
Eisenhower material added in 1960 ed.

86.   Anderson, Patrick.   The Presidents' Men: White House
      Assistants of Franklin D. Roosevelt, Harry S. Truman,
Dwight D. Eisenhower, John F. Kennedy and Lyndon B.
Johnson.   Garden City: Doubleday, 1968.

87.   Bailey, Thomas A.   Presidential Greatness: The Image
      and the Man from George Washington to the Present.
New York: Appleton-Century, 1966.

88.   Bell, Jack.   The Splendid Misery: The Story of the
      Presidency and Power Politics at Close Range.   Gar-
den City: Doubleday, 1960.

89.   Burns, James McGregor.   Presidential Government:
      The Crucible of Leadership.   Boston: Houghton Mifflin,
1965.

90.   Cornwell, Elmer E.   Presidential Leadership of Public
      Opinion.   Bloomington: Indiana University Press, 1965.

91.   Cronin, Thomas E. and Greenberg, Sanford D. , eds.
      The Presidential Advisory System.   New York: Har-
per & Row, 1969.

92.   Cummings, Milton C.   Congressmen and the Electorate:
      Elections for the U. S. House and the President, 1920-
1964.   New York: The Free Press, 1966.

93.   Fenno, Richard F.   The President's Cabinet: An
      Analysis in the Period from Wilson to Eisenhower.
Cambridge: Harvard University Press, 1959.

94.   Finer, Herman.   The Presidency: Crisis and Regener-
      ation: An Essay in Possibilities.   Chicago: University
of Chicago Press, 1960.

95.   Henry, Laurin L.   Presidential Transitions.   Washing-
      ton: Brookings Institution, 1960.

96.   Hobbs, Edward H.   Behind the President: A Study of
      Executive Office Agencies.   Washington: Public Affairs
Press, 1954.

97.   James, Dorothy Buckton.   The Contemporary Presi-
      dency.   New York: Pegasus, 1969.

98.   Johnson, Walter.   1600 Pennsylvania Avenue: Presidents

and the People, 1929-1959. Boston: Little, Brown,
1960.

99. Kallenbach, Joseph E. The American Chief Execu-
     tive: The Presidency and the Governorship. New
York: Harper & Row, 1966.

100. Kramer, Robert, and Marcuse, Herman, "Executive
      Privilege: A Study of the Period 1953-1960," George
Washington Law Review, XXIX, (April, June, 1961), 623-
717, 827-916.

101. Landecker, Manfred. The President and Public
      Opinion: Leadership in Foreign Affairs. Washington:
Public Affairs Press, 1969.

102. Longaker, Richard P. The Presidency and Individual
      Liberties. Ithaca: Cornell University Press, 1961.

103. May, Ernest R. , ed. The Ultimate Decision: The
      President as Commander in Chief. New York:
Braziller, 1960.

104. Mueller, John E. , "Presidential Popularity from
      Truman to Johnson," American Political Science
Review, LXIV (March, 1970), 18-34.

105. Neustadt, Richard E. , "The Presidency and Legisla-
      tion: Planning the President's Program," American
Political Science Review, XLIX (December, 1955), 980-1021.

106. _____. "The Presidency and Legislation: The
      Growth of Central Clearance," American Political
Science Review, XLVIII (September, 1954), 641-71.

107. _____. Presidential Power: The Politics of
      Leadership. New York: Wiley, 1969.

108. Pollard, James E. The Presidents and the Press:
      Truman to Johnson. Washington: Public Affairs
Press, 1964.

109. Rossiter, Clinton L. The American Presidency.
      New York: Harcourt, Brace, 1956.

110. Smith, John Malcolm and Cotter, Cornelius P.
      Powers of the President during Crises. Washington:

Public Affairs Press, 1960.

111. Steelman, John R. and Kreager, H. Dewayne, "The
      Executive Office As Administrative Coordinator,"
Law and Contemporary Problems, XXI (Autumn, 1956),
688-709.

112. Tugwell, Rexford G. The Enlargement of the Presi-
      dency. Garden City: Doubleday, 1960.

                    C. THE CONGRESS

1. General

113. Bailey, Stephen K. and Samuel, Howard D. Congress
      at Work. New York: Holt, 1952.

114. _____. Congress Makes a Law: The Story behind
      the Employment Act of 1946. New York: Columbia
University Press, 1950.

115. Bolling, Richard. Power in the House: A History of
      the Leadership of the House of Representatives. New
York: Dutton, 1968.

116. Clark, Joseph S. Congress: The Sapless Branch.
      New York: Harper & Row, 1964.

117. _____, and others. The Senate Establishment.
      New York: Hill & Wang, 1963.

118. Clausen, Aage R. and Cheney, Richard B., "A Com-
      parative Analysis of Senate-House Voting on Economic
and Welfare Policy, 1953-1964," American Political Science
Review, LXIV (March, 1970), 138-52.

119. Congressional Quarterly Service, Washington, D.C.
      Congress and the Nation, 1945-1964: A Review of
Government and Politics in the Postwar Years. Washington: Congressional Quarterly Service, 1965.

120. _____. Congressional Reform: An Examination of
      the Operation, Rules and Customs of Congress and
Proposals for Revision. Washington: Congressional Quarterly Service, 1964.

121.   Dahl, Robert Alan.   Congress and Foreign Policy.
        New York: Harcourt, Brace, 1950.

122.   Farnsworth, David Nelson.   The Senate Committee
        on Foreign Relations.   Urbana: University of Illinois
Press, 1961.   (Illinois Studies in the Social Sciences, v.
49).

123.   Fenno, Richard F., "The House Appropriations Com-
        mittee As a Political System: The Problem of Inte-
gration," American Political Science Review, LVI (June,
1962), 310-324.

124.   Galloway, George B.   Congress at the Crossroads.
        New York: Crowell, 1946.

125.   Griffith, Ernest Stacey.   Congress: Its Contemporary
        Role.   4th ed.   New York: New York University
Press, 1967.   First published 1951.

126.   Hartmann, Susan M.   Truman and the 80th Congress.
        Columbia: University of Missouri Press, 1971.

127.   Huitt, Ralph K., "Democratic Party Leadership in
        the Senate," American Political Science Review, LV
(June, 1961), 333-344.

128.   _____, and Peabody, Robert L.   Congress: Two
        Decades of Analysis.   New York: Harper & Row,
1969.

129.   Jewell, Malcolm E.   Senatorial Politics & Foreign
        Policy.   Lexington: University of Kentucky Press,
1962.

130.   Marwell, Gerald, "Party, Region and the Dimensions
        of Conflict in the House of Representatives, 1949-
1954," American Political Science Review, LXI (June, 1967),
380-399.

131.   Matthews, Donald R.   Senators and Their World.
        Chapel Hill: University of North Carolina Press,
1960.

132.   Milbrath, Lester W.   The Washington Lobbyists.
        Chicago: Rand McNally, 1963.

133. Murphy, Walter F. <u>Congress and the Court: A Case</u>
      <u>Study in the American Political Process</u>. Chicago:
University of Chicago Press, 1962.

134. Neustadt, Richard E. , "Congress and the Fair Deal:
      A Legislative Balance Sheet," <u>Public Policy</u>, V (1954),
349-81.

135. Peabody, Robert L. and Polsby, Nelson W. , eds.
      <u>New Perspectives on the House of Representatives</u>.
Chicago: Rand McNally, 1963.

136. Pritchett, C. Herman. <u>Congress versus the Supreme</u>
      <u>Court, 1957-1960</u>. Minneapolis: University of Minne-
sota Press, 1961.

137. Riddick, Floyd M. , "The Eighty-first Congress: First
      and Second Sessions," <u>Western Political Quarterly</u>,
IV (March, 1951), 48-66.

138. _____. , "The Eighty-second Congress: First Ses-
      sion," <u>Western Political Quarterly</u>, V (March, 1952),
94-108.

139. Riddle, Donald H. <u>The Truman Committee: A Study</u>
      <u>in Congressional Responsibility</u>. New Brunswick,
N. J. , Rutgers University Press, 1964.

140. Ridgeway, Marian E. <u>The Missouri Basin's Pick-</u>
      <u>Sloan: A Case Study in Congressional Determination</u>.
Urbana: University of Illinois Press, 1955. (Illinois
Studies in the Social Sciences, v. 35).

141. Robinson, James A. <u>Congress and Foreign Policy-</u>
      <u>Making: A Study in Legislative Influence and Initiative</u>.
Rev. ed. Homewood, Ill. , Dorsey Press, 1967.

142. Schriftgiesser, Karl. <u>The Lobbyists: The Art and</u>
      <u>Business of Influencing Lawmakers</u>. Boston: Little,
Brown, 1951.

143. Scoble, Harry M. <u>Ideology and Electoral Action: A</u>
      <u>Comparative Study of the National Committee for an</u>
<u>Effective Congress</u>. San Francisco: Chandler Publishing
Company, 1967.

144. Shannon, W. Wayne. <u>Party Constituency, and</u>

Congressional Voting: A Study of Legislative Behavior
in the United States House of Representatives. Baton Rouge:
Louisiana State University Press, 1968.

145.   Truman, David B. , ed. The Congress and America's
       Future. Englewood Cliffs, N. J. , Prentice-Hall, 1965.

146.   Truman, David B. The Congressional Party: A Case
       Study. New York: Wiley, 1959.

147.   White, William S. Citadel: The Story of the United
       States Senate. New York: Harper, 1957.

2.   Statehood: Alaska and Hawaii

148.   "Alaska's Flickering Star," [Statehood for the Islands
       of Hawaii] Economist, CLXXXVII (April 26, 1958),
309-310.

149.   Atwood, Robert Bruce, "Alaska's Struggle for State-
       hood," State Government, XXXI (Fall, 1958), 202-208.

150.   Dill, William C. Statehood for Hawaii. Philadelphia:
       Dorrance, 1949.

151.   Gruening, Ernest Henry. The Battle for Alaska
       Statehood. College: University of Alaska Press,
distributed by the University of Washington Press, Seattle,
1967.

152.   _____, "Statehood for Alaska," Harpers Magazine,
       CCVI (May, 1953), 72-77.

153.   [Hawaii] State Government, XXXII (Summer, 1959),
       146-161. Contents: "Hawaii, The Aloha State," by
W. F. Quinn; "Statehood and Hawaii's People," by J. A.
Burns; "What Statehood Means to Hawaii," by R. M.
Kamins.

154.   Hunter, Charles H. , "Congress and Statehood for
       Hawaii," World Affairs Quarterly, XXIX (January,
1959), 354-378.

155.   Kinevan, Marcos E. , "Alaska and Hawaii: From
       Territoriality to Statehood," California Law Review,
XXXVIII (June, 1950), 273-292.

156.   Stewart, Thomas B.   "The Meaning of Statehood to
       Alaska," State Government, XXXI (Fall, 1958), 215-
219.

157.   U. S. Congress.   House.   Committee on Public Lands.
       Subcommittee on Territorial and Insular Possessions.
Statehood for Alaska.   Hearings, March 4 and 8, 1949.
Washington: Government Printing Office, 1949.   (81st Con-
gress, 1st Session).

158.   _____. _____. Committee on the Territories.
       Statehood for Hawaii.   Hearings, January 7-18, 1946.
Washington: Government Printing Office, 1946.   (79th Congress, 2d Session).

159.   _____. Senate.   Committee on Interior and Insular
       Affairs.   Alaska Statehood.   Hearings, April 24-29,
1950.   Washington: Government Printing Office, 1950.
(81st Congress, 2d Session).

160.   _____. _____. _____. Hawaii Statehood.
       Hearings, May 1-5, 1950.   Washington: Government
Printing Office, 1950.   (81st Congress, 2d Session).

161.   _____. _____. _____. Subcommittee on
       Territories and Insular Affairs.   Statehood for Hawaii.
Hearing, March 6, 1953.   Washington: Government Printing
Office, 1953.   (83d Congress, 1st Session).

162.   Wilbur, Ray Lyman, "Statehood for Hawaii," Atlantic
       Monthly, CLXVI (October, 1940), 494-497.

D.   THE SUPREME COURT

163.   Bartholomew, Paul C. , "The Supreme Court of the
       United States, 1946-1956," Southwestern Social Science
Quarterly, XXXVIII (December, 1957), 195-205.

164.   Black, Hugo Lafayette.   One Man's Fight for Freedom:
       Mr. Justice Black and the Bill of Rights: A Collection
of Supreme Court Opinions.   New York: Knopf, 1963.

165.   Brown, Oliver.   Argument; Argument: The Oral Argu-
       ment before the Supreme Court in Brown v. Board
of Education of Topeka, 1951-55.   New York: Chelsea
House Publishers, 1969.

166.   Clark, Tom C. and Perlman, Philip B.   Prejudice
       and Property: An Historic Brief against Racial
Covenants Submitted to the Supreme Court by Tom C. Clark,
Attorney General of the U. S. and Philip B. Perlman, Soli-
citor General of the U. S. Washington: Public Affairs Press,
1948.

167.   Friedman, Leon and Israel, Fred L. eds.   The Jus-
       tices of the United States Supreme Court, 1789-1969:
Their Lives and Their Major Opinions.   New York: Chelsea
House Publishers in Association with R. R. Bowker, 1969.

168.   Jackson, Percival E.   Dissent in the Supreme Court:
       A Chronology.   Norman: University of Oklahoma
Press, 1969.

169.   Jackson, Robert H.   Dispassionate Justice: A Syn-
       thesis of the Judicial Opinions of Robert H. Jackson.
Indianapolis: Bobbs-Merrill, 1969.

170.   Landynski, Jacob W.   Search and Seizure and the
       Supreme Court: A Study in Constitutional Interpreta-
tion.   Baltimore: Johns Hopkins Press, 1966.

171.   Mason, Alpheus Thomas.   The Supreme Court from
       Taft to Warren.   Baton Rouge: Louisiana State
University Press, 1958.

172.   Murphy, Walter F.   Congress and the Court: A Case
       Study in the American Political Process.   Chicago:
University of Chicago Press, 1962.

173.   Pritchett, C. Herman.   Congress versus the Supreme
       Court, 1957-1960.   Minneapolis: University of
Minnesota Press, 1961.

174.   Schubert, Glendon A.   The Judicial Mind: The Atti-
       tudes and Ideologies of Supreme Court Justices, 1946-
1963.   Evanston: Northwestern University Press, 1965.

175.   Thomas, Helen Shirley.   Felix Frankfurter: Scholar
       on the Bench.   Baltimore: Johns Hopkins Press,
1960.

176.   Warren, Earl.   The Public Papers of Chief Justice
       Earl Warren.   New York: Simon and Schuster, 1959.

177.   Westin, Alan F. , ed.   An Autobiography of the
       Supreme Court: Off-the-Bench Commentary by the
Justices.   New York: Macmillan, 1963.

E.   ELECTIONS

178.   Abels, Jules.   Out of the Jaws of Victory.   New
       York: Holt, 1959.

179.   Ader, Emile B. , "Why the Dixiecrats Failed," Journal
       of Politics, XV (August, 1953), 356-369.

180.   Bartley, Numan V.   From Thurmond to Wallace:
       Political Tendencies in Georgia, 1948-1968.   Balti-
more: Johns Hopkins Press, 1970.

181.   Berelson, Bernard, Lazarsfeld, Paul F. , and McPhee,
       William N.   Voting: A Study of Opinion Formation in
a Presidential Campaign.   Chicago: University of Chicago
Press, 1954.

182.   Blanchard, Robert, Meyer, Richard, and Morley,
       Blaine.   Presidential Elections, 1948-1960.   Salt
Lake City: Institute of Government, University of Utah,
1961.   (Research Monograph No. 4)

183.   Brown, John Mason.   Through These Men: Some As-
       pects of Our Passing History.   New York: Harper,
1956.

184.   Burdick, Eugene and Brodbeck, Arthur J.   American
       Voting Behavior.   Glencoe, Ill. :   Free Press, 1959.

185.   Busch, Noel F.   Adlai E. Stevenson of Illinois: A
       Portrait.   New York: Farrar, Straus & Young, 1952.

186.   Calkins, Fay.   The CIO and the Democratic Party.
       Chicago: University of Chicago Press, 1952.

187.   Campbell, Angus, and others.   The American Voter.
       New York: Wiley, 1960.

188.   _____, _____.   Elections and the Political
       Order.   New York: Wiley, 1966.   (Survey Research
Center, Institute for Social Research, the University of
Michigan)

189. _____, Gurin, Gerald, and Miller, Warren E.
      "Political Issues and the Voter, November, 1952,"
American Political Science Review, XLVII (June, 1953),
359-385.

190. Cochran, Bert. Adlai Stevenson: Patrician among the
      Politicians. New York: Funk & Wagnalls, 1969.

191. Cummings, Milton C. Congressmen and the Elec-
      torate: Elections for the U.S. House and the Presi-
dent, 1920-1964. New York: Free Press, 1966.

192. David, Paul T., Moos, Malcolm, and Goldman,
      Ralph M. Presidential Nominating Politics in 1952.
Baltimore: Johns Hopkins Press, 1954. 5 vols.

193. Davis, James W. Presidential Primaries: Road to
      the White House. New York: Crowell, 1967.

194. Davis, Kenneth S. A Prophet in His Own Country:
      The Triumphs and Defeats of Adlai E. Stevenson.
Garden City: Doubleday, 1957.

195. De Santis, Vincent P., "The Presidential Election of
      1952," Review of Politics, XV (April, 1953), 131-
150.

196. Divine, Robert A., "The Cold War and the Election
      of 1948," Journal of American History, LIX (June,
1972), 90-110.

197. Eaton, Herbert. Presidential Timber: A History of
      Nominating Conventions, 1868-1960. New York:
Free Press of Glencoe, 1964.

198. Eldersveld, Samuel J., "The Influence of Metropolitan
      Party Pluralities in Presidential Elections Since 1920:
A Study of Twelve Key Cities," American Political Science
Review, XLIII (December, 1949), 1189-1206.

199. Ernst, Morris L. and Loth, David. The People
      Know Best: The Ballot vs. the Polls. Washington:
Public Affairs Press, 1949.

200. Eulau, Heinz. Class and Party in the Eisenhower
      Years: Class Roles and Perspectives in the 1952 and
1956 Elections. New York: Free Press of Glencoe, 1962.

201. Garson, Robert A., "The Alienation of the South: A
     Crisis for Harry S. Truman and the Democratic
Party, 1945-1948," Missouri Historical Review, LXIV (July,
1970), 448-471.

202. Harris, Louis. Is There a Republican Majority?
     Political Trends, 1952-1956. New York: Harper,
1956.

203. Heard, Alexander. A Two-Party South? Chapel Hill:
     University of North Carolina Press, 1952.

204. Johnson, Walter. How We Drafted Adlai Stevenson.
     New York: Knopf, 1955.

205. Key, Vladimir O. and Cummings, Milton C. The
     Responsible Electorate: Rationality in Presidential
Voting, 1936-1960. Cambridge: Harvard University Press,
1966.

206. _____, and Heard, Alexander. Southern Politics
     in State and Nation. New York: Knopf, 1949.

207. Lee, R. Alton, "The Truman-80th Congress Struggle
     over Tax Policy," Historian, XXXIII (November,
1970), 68-82.

208. _____, "The Turnip Session of the Do-Nothing
     Congress: Presidential Campaign Strategy," South-
western Social Science Quarterly, (December, 1963), 256-
267.

209. Leeds, Morton, "The AFL in the 1948 Elections,"
     Social Research, XVII (June, 1950), 207-18.

210. Lemmon, Sarah McCulloh, "Ideology of the 'Dixiecrat'
     Movement," Social Forces, XXX (December, 1951),
162-171.

211. Lubell, Samuel, "Who Really Elected Truman?"
     Saturday Evening Post, CCXXI (January 22, 1949),
15-17, 54-64.

212. McCarthy, Eugene J. A Liberal Answer to the Con-
     servative Challenge. New York: Praeger, 1965.

213. Macdonald, Dwight. Henry Wallace: The Man and

the Myth. New York: Vanguard, 1948.

214. MacDougall, Curtis D. Gideon's Army. New York: Marzani & Munsell, 1965-1966. 3 vols.

215. Martin, John B. Adlai Stevenson. New York: Harper, 1952.

216. Muller, Herbert J. Adlai Stevenson: A Study in Values. New York: Harper & Row, 1967.

217. Redding, John M. (Jack). Inside the Democratic Party. Indianapolis: Bobbs-Merrill, 1958.

218. Roseboom, Eugene H. A History of Presidential Elections from George Washington to Richard M. Nixon. 3d ed. New York: Macmillan, 1970.

219. Ross, Irwin. The Loneliest Campaign: The Truman Victory of 1948. New York: New American Library, 1968.

220. Schapsmeier, Edgar L. and Schapsmeier, Frederick H. Prophet in Politics: Henry A. Wallace and the War Years, 1940-1965. Ames: Iowa State University Press, 1970.

221. Schlesinger, Arthur M., Israel, Fred L., and Hansen, William P., eds. History of American Presidential Elections. New York: Chelsea House, 1971. 4 vols. Vol. IV: 1940-1968.

222. Schmidt, Karl M. Henry A. Wallace: Quixotic Crusade, 1948. Syracuse: Syracuse University Press, 1960.

223. Shannon, David A. The Decline of American Communism: A History of the Communist Party of the United States Since 1945. New York: Harcourt, Brace and World, 1959.

224. Shogan, Robert, "1948 Election," American Heritage, XIX (June, 1968), 22-31, 104-111.

225. Sitkoff, Harvard, "Harry Truman and the Election of 1948: The Coming of Age of Civil Rights in American Politics," Journal of Southern History, XXXVII (November, 1971), 597-616.

226. Stevenson, Adlai E. Adlai Stevenson's Public Years, with Text from His Speeches and Writings. New York: Grossman Publishers, 1966.

227. _____. Major Campaign Speeches, 1952. New York: Random House, 1953.

228. _____. The New America. New York: Harper, 1957.

229. _____. Speeches, New York: Random House, 1952.

230. _____. What I Think. New York: Harper, 1956.

231. Thomson, Charles A. H. and Shattuck, Frances M. The 1956 Presidential Campaign. Washington: Brookings Institution, 1960.

232. Wallace, Henry A. Toward World Peace. New York: Reynal & Hitchcock, 1948.

233. White, Theodore H. The Making of the President, 1960. New York: Atheneum, 1961.

234. Williams, Oliver P. "The Commodity Credit Corporation and the 1948 Presidential Election," Midwest Journal of Political Science, I (August, 1957), 111-124.

F. THE TRUMAN ADMINISTRATION

1. General

235. Abels, Jules. The Truman Scandals. Chicago: Regnery, 1956.

236. Allen, Robert S. and Shannon, William V. The Truman Merry-Go-Round. New York: Vanguard Press, 1950.

237. Berman, William C. The Politics of Civil Rights in the Truman Administration. Columbus: Ohio State University Press, 1970.

238. Bernstein, Barton J., ed. Politics and Policies of the Truman Administration. Chicago: Quadrangle Books, 1970.

239.   Bernstein, Barton J. , "The Presidency under Tru-
       man," Yale Political Review, IV (Fall, 1964), 8-9, 24.

240.   _____. , and Matusow, Allen J. , eds.   The Tru-
       man Administration: A Documentary History.   New
York: Harper & Row, 1966.

241.   _____. , "Truman's Record," Progressive, XXX
       (October, 1966), 46-48.

242.   Brooks, Philip C. , "Understanding the Presidency:
       The Harry S. Truman Library," Prologue: Journal
of the National Archives, I (Winter, 1969), 3-12.

243.   Coffin, Tristram. Missouri Compromise. Boston:
       Little, Brown, 1947.

244.   Davies, Richard O. Housing Reform during the
       Truman Administration. Columbia: University of
Missouri Press, 1966.

245.   Druks, Herbert. Harry S. Truman and the Russians,
       1945-1953. New York: Speller, 1967.

246.   Freeland, Richard M. The Truman Doctrine and the
       Origins of McCarthyism: Foreign Policy, Domestic
Politics, and Internal Security, 1946-1948. New York:
Knopf, 1972.

247.   Gross, Bertram M. and Lewis, John P. , "The
       President's Economic Staff during the Truman Ad-
ministration," American Political Science Review, XLVIII
(March, 1954), 114-130.

248.   Gunther, John. Inside U. S. A. Rev. ed.   New York:
       Harper, 1951. First published 1947.

249.   Hamby, Alonzo L. , "The Liberals, Truman, and
       FDR As Symbol and Myth," Journal of American
History, LVI (March, 1970), 859-867.

250.   _____. , "The Vital Center, the Fair Deal, and the
       Quest for a Liberal Political Economy," American
Historical Review, LXXVII (June, 1972), 653-678.

251.   Hartmann, Susan M. Truman and the 80th Congress.
       Columbia: University of Missouri Press, 1971.

252.   Hersey, John, "Profiles: Mr. President, III - Forty-
       eight Hours," New Yorker, XXVII (April 21, 1951),
36-60.

253.   Kirkendall, Richard S. , ed.   The Truman Period As a
       Research Field.   Columbia: University of Missouri
Press, 1967.   Papers from a conference held in the Truman Library in April 1966.

254.   Koenig, Louis W. , ed.   The Truman Administration:
       Its Principles and Practice.   New York: New York
University Press, 1956.

255.   _____.   "Truman's Global Leadership," Current
       History, XXXIX (October, 1960), 225-229.

256.   Lee, R. Alton.   Truman and Taft-Hartley: A Question
       of Mandate.   Lexington: University of Kentucky Press,
1966.

257.   Lorenz, A. L. , "Truman and the Press Conference,"
       Journalism Quarterly, XLIII (Winter, 1966), 671-679,
708.

258.   McClure, Arthur F.   The Truman Administration
       and the Problems of Post-War Labor, 1945-1948.
Rutherford, N. J. : Fairleigh Dickinson University Press,
1969.

259.   Madison, Charles A.   Leaders and Liberals in 20th
       Century America.   New York: Ungar, 1961.

260.   Morgan, H. Wayne.   "History and the Presidency:
       Harry S. Truman," Phylon Quarterly, XIX (July,
1958), 162-170.

261.   Phillips, Cabell B. H.   The Truman Presidency:
       The History of a Triumphant Succession.   New York:
Macmillan, 1966.

262.   Pollard, James E. , "Truman and the Press: Final
       Phase, 1951-53," Journalism Quarterly, XXX (Sum-
mer, 1953), 273-286.

263.   Quade, Quentin L. , "The Truman Administration and
       the Separation of Power: The Case of the Marshall
Plan," Review of Politics, XXVII (January, 1965), 58-77.

264. Sawyer, Charles. Concerns of a Conservative Demo-
      crat. Carbondale: Southern Illinois University Press,
1968.

265. Steelman, John R. , and Kreager, H. Dewayne, "The
      Executive Office as Administrative Coordinator," Law
and Contemporary Problems, XXI (Autumn, 1956), 688-709.

266. Theoharis, Athan, "The Truman Presidency: Trial
      and Error," Wisconsin Magazine of History, LV
(Autumn, 1971).

267. Truman, Harry S. The Memoirs of Harry Truman.
      Garden City: Doubleday, 1955-56. Vol. I, Year of
Decisions. Vol. II, Years of Trial and Hope.

268. _____. Mr. President, compiled by William Hill-
      man. New York: Farrar, Straus & Young, 1952.

269. _____. The Truman Program: Addresses and
      Messages, ed. by Morris Schnapper. Washington:
Public Affairs Press, 1949.

270. _____. Truman Speaks. [Lectures and discus-
      sions held at Columbia University on April 27, 28,
and 29, 1959.] New York: Columbia University Press,
1960.

271. Truman Library Institute for National and Inter-
      national Affairs. Conference of Scholars on the
Truman Administration and Civil Rights, April 5-6, 1968.
Independence, Mo. , Author, 1968. Mimeographed.

272. U. S. President. Public Papers of the Presidents:
      Harry S. Truman, 1945-1953. Washington: Govern-
ment Printing Office, 1961-1966. 8 vols.

2. Biographies of Truman

273. Daniels, Jonathan. The Man of Independence. Phila-
      delphia: Lippincott, 1950.

274. McNaughton, Frank and Hehmeyer, Walter. This
      Man Truman. New York: McGraw-Hill, 1945.

275. _____. _____. Harry Truman, President.
New York: McGraw-Hill, 1948.

276.   Powell, Eugene James (Gene).   Tom's Boy Harry:
       The First Complete Authentic Story of Harry Tru-
man's Connection with the Pendergast Machine.   Jefferson
City, Mo. :   Hawthorn Publishing Co. , 1948.

277.   Steinberg, Alfred.   The Man from Missouri: The
       Life and Times of Harry S. Truman.   New York:
Putnam's, 1962.

278.   Truman, Margaret with Cousins, Margaret.   ...
       Souvenir.   New York: McGraw-Hill, 1956.   At head
of title: Margaret Truman's Own Story.

G.   THE EISENHOWER ADMINISTRATION

1.   General

279.   Adams, Sherman.   Firsthand Report: The Story of
       the Eisenhower Administration.   New York: Harper,
1961.

280.   Albertson, Dean, ed.   Eisenhower As President.
       New York: Hill and Wang, 1963.

281.   Branyan, Robert L. and Larsen, Lawrence H. eds.
       The Eisenhower Administration: 1953-1961.   A Docu-
mentary History.   New York: Random House, 1971.

282.   Buckley, William F. , "The Tranquil World of Dwight
       D. Eisenhower," National Review, V (January 18,
1958), 57-59.

283.   Childs, Marquis W.   Eisenhower, Captive Hero: A
       Critical Study of the General and the President.   New
York: Harcourt, Brace, 1958.

284.   Cutler, Robert.   No Time for Rest.   Boston: Little,
       Brown, 1966.

285.   Donovan, Robert J.   Eisenhower: The Inside Story.
       New York: Harper, 1956.

286.   Eisenhower, Dwight David.   The Papers of Dwight
       David Eisenhower: The War Years.   Baltimore:
Johns Hopkins Press, 1970.

287. _____ . Peace with Justice: Selected Addresses.
       New York: Columbia University Press, 1961.

288. _____ . The Quotable Dwight D. Eisenhower,
       comp. and ed. by Elsie Gollagher. Anderson, S. C. :
Droke House, Publishers. Distributed by Grosset and Dunlap, 1967.

289. _____ . The White House Years. Garden City:
       Doubleday, 1963-1965. 2 vols. Vol. I Mandate for
Change, 1953-1956. Vol. II Waging Peace, 1956-1961.

290. Frier, David A. Conflict of Interest in the Eisen-
       hower Administration. Ames: Iowa State University
Press, 1969.

291. Graebner, Norman A. , "Eisenhower's Popular Lea-
       dership," Current History, XXXIX (October, 1960),
230-236, 244.

292. Hauge, Gabriel, "Economics of Eisenhower Dynamic
       Conservatism," Commercial and Financial Chronicle,
CLXXXII (October 27, 1955), 1749, 1776-1777.

293. Holmans, A. E. "The Eisenhower Administration
       and the Recession, 1953-1955," Oxford Economic
Papers, n. s. , X (February, 1958), 34-54.

294. Hughes, Emmet John. The Ordeal of Power: A
       Political Memoir of the Eisenhower Years. New
York: Atheneum, 1963.

295. Kempton, Murray, "The Underestimation of Dwight
       D. Eisenhower," Esquire, LXVIII (September, 1967),
108-109, 156.

296. Kramer, Robert and Marcuse, Herman, "Executive
       Privilege: A Study of the Period 1953-1960," George
Washington Law Review, XXIX (April, June, 1961), 623-717,
827-916.

297. Larson, Arthur. Eisenhower: The President Nobody
       Knew. New York: Scribner's, 1968.

298. Miller, William J. Henry Cabot Lodge: A Biography.
       New York: Heineman, 1967.

299. Miller, William Lee. Piety along the Potomac:

      Notes on Politics and Morals in the Fifties.   Boston:
Houghton Mifflin, 1964.

300. Morrow, E. Frederic. Black Man in the White
      House: A Diary of the Eisenhower Years by the
Administrative Officer for Special Projects.   New York:
Coward-McCann, 1963.

301. Murphy, Charles J. V. , "The Budget and Eisenhower,"
      Fortune, LVI (July, 1957), 96-99, 228-30.

302. _____. , "The Eisenhower Shift," Fortune, LIII
      (January, 1956), 82-87, 206-208.

303. _____. , "Eisenhower's White House," Fortune,
      XLVIII (July, 1953), 75 ff.

304. _____. , "The White House Since Sputnik," For-
      tune, LVII (January, 1958).

305. Neustadt, Richard E.   "The Presidency and Legis-
      lation: The Growth of Central Clearance," American
Political Science Review, XLVIII (September, 1954), 641-
671.

306. _____. , "The Presidency and Legislation: Planning
      the President's Program," American Political Science
Review, XLIX (December, 1955), 980-1021.

307. Niebuhr, Reinhold, "The Eisenhower Era," The New
      Leader, XLIII (October 3, 1960), 3-4.

308. Nixon, Richard M.   Six Crises.   Garden City:
      Doubleday, 1962.

309. Pollard, James E. , "Eisenhower and the Press: The
      Final Phase," Journalism Quarterly, XXXVIII (Spring,
1961), 181-186.

310. _____. , "Eisenhower and the Press: The First
      Two Years," Journalism Quarterly, XXXII (Summer,
1955) 285-300.

311. Pusey, Merlo J. Eisenhower, the President.   New
      York: Macmillan, 1956.

312. Rovere, Richard H. Affairs of State: The Eisenhower

Years. New York: Farrar, Straus and Cudahy, 1956.

313.   ., "Eisenhower over the Shoulder," American Scholar, XXXI (Spring, 1962), 176-179.

314.   ., "Eisenhower Revisited--A Political Genius? A Brilliant Man? New York Times Magazine, February 7, 1971, p. 14-15+.

315. Scher, Seymour, "Regulatory Agency Control through Appointment: The Case of the Eisenhower Administration and the NLRB," Journal of Politics, XXIII (November, 1961), 667-688.

316. Shannon, William V., "Eisenhower As President: A Critical Appraisal of the Record," Commentary, XXVI (November, 1958), 390-398.

317. Shoemaker, Ralph Joseph. The Presidents Words, an Index. Louisville, Ky.: E. DeG. Shoemaker and R. J. Shoemaker, 1954-1961. 7 vols.

318. Smith, A. Merriman. Meet Mr. Eisenhower. New York: Harper, 1955.

319. U.S. Congress. House of Representatives. Selected Speeches of Dwight David Eisenhower, 34th President of the United States. Washington: Government Printing Office, 1970. (91st Congress, 2d Session, House Document 91355).

320. U.S. President. Public Papers of the Presidents: Dwight D. Eisenhower, 1953-1961. Washington: Government Printing Office, 1960-1961. 8 vols.

321. Vexler, Robert I., ed. Dwight D. Eisenhower, 1890-1969: Chronology, Documents, Bibliographical Aids. Dobbs Ferry, N.Y.: Oceana Publications, 1970.

2.   The Federal Aid Highway Act (1956)

322. Hillenbrand, Bernard F., "Challenge for Cities: Federal Highway Program Gives Opportunity to Ease Traffic Choked Areas," National Municipal Review, XLV (November, 1956), 488-493.

323. Howard, John Tasker, "Metropolitan Planning and the

        Federal Highway Program," American City, LXXII
(June, 1957), 225.

324.   Martin, James Walter, "Administrative Dangers in
       the Enlarged Highway Program," Public Administra-
tion Review, XIX (Summer, 1959), 164-172.

325.   Moses, Robert, "The New Super-Highways: Blessing
       or Blight?" Harper's Magazine, CCXIII (December,
1956), 27-31.

326.   "President's Highway Program: Background Material
       and Pro and Con Discussion," Congressional Digest,
XXXIV (May, 1955), 131-160.

327.   U. S. Congress. House. Committee on Public Works.
       Subcommittee on Roads. National Highway Program:
Federal Aid Highway Act of 1956. Hearings, February 7 to
March 5, 1956. Washington: Government Printing Office,
1956. (84th Congress, 2d Session).

328.   _____. _____. Committee on Ways and Means.
       Highway Revenue Act of 1956. Hearings, February
14-21, 1956. Washington: Government Printing Office,
1956. (84th Congress, 2d Session).

329.   _____. Senate. Committee on Finance. Highway
       Revenue Act: Hearings, May 17-18, 1956. Washing-
ton: Government Printing Office, 1956. (84th Congress,
2d Session).

330.   _____. _____. Committee on Public Works.
       Progress and Status of the National Highway Program.
Hearings January 7-April 2, 1957. Washington: Government Printing Office, 1957. (85th Congress, 1st Session).

3.   Biographies of Eisenhower

331.   Eisenhower, Dwight David. At Ease: Stories I Tell
       to Friends. Garden City: Doubleday, 1967.

332.   _____. In Review: Pictures I've Kept: A Concise
       Pictorial "Autobiography." New York: Doubleday,
1969.

333.   _____. What Eisenhower Thinks. New York:
       Crowell, 1952.

334.   Eisenhower, American Hero: The Historical Record
       of His Life, by the Editors of American Heritage
Magazine and United Press International.   New York:
American Heritage, 1969.

335.   Gunther, John.   Eisenhower: The Man and the Sym-
       bol.   New York: Harper, 1952.

336.   Morin, Relman.   Dwight D. Eisenhower: A Gauge of
       Greatness.   New York: Simon & Schuster, 1969.

337.   National Cartoonists Society.   President Eisenhower's
       Cartoon Book, by 95 of America's Leading Cartoonists,
Members of the National Cartoonists Society.   New York:
Published in conjunction with the United States Savings Bonds
Program by F. Fell, 1956.

338.   Smith, A. Merriman.   A President's Odyssey.   New
       York: Harper & Row, 1961.

339.   Snyder, Marty and Kittler, Glenn.   My Friend Ike.
       New York: Fell, 1956.

340.   U. S. Congress.   House of Representatives.   Memorial
       Services in the Congress of the United States and Tri-
butes in Eulogy of Dwight David Eisenhower.   Washington:
Government Printing Office, 1970.   (91st Congress, 1st
Session, House Document No. 91-195).

III. AMERICAN FOREIGN POLICY

A. GENERAL

341. Acheson, Dean, "Foreign Policy and Presidential Moralism," Reporter, XVI (May 2, 1957), 10-14.

342. _____. The Pattern of Responsibility. Ed. by McGeorge Bundy from the record of Secretary of State Dean Acheson. Boston: Houghton Mifflin, 1952.

343. _____. Power and Diplomacy. Cambridge: Harvard University Press, 1958.

344. _____. Present at the Creation: My Years in the State Department. New York: Norton, 1969.

345. _____. Sketches from Life of Men I Have Known. New York: Harper, 1961.

346. Adler, Selig. The Isolationist Impulse: Its Twentieth Century Reaction. New York: Abelard-Schuman, 1957.

347. Agar, Herbert. The Price of Power: America Since 1945. Chicago: University of Chicago Press, 1957.

348. Almond, Gabriel A. The American People and Foreign Policy. 2nd ed. New York: Praeger, 1960.

349. Alsop, Joseph and Alsop, Stewart. The Reporter's Trade. New York: Reynal, 1958.

350. "American Foreign Policy--Freedoms and Restraints," Daedalus, XCI (Fall, 1962). Entire issue.

351. Appleton, Sheldon. United States Foreign Policy: An Introduction, with Cases. Boston: Little, Brown, 1968.

352. Armstrong, John P. , "The Enigma of Senator Taft

and American Foreign Policy," Review of Politics,
XVII (April, 1955), 206-231.

353. Bailey, Thomas A. The Art of Diplomacy: The
      American Experience. New York: Appleton-Century-
Crofts, 1968.

354. _____. The Man in the Street: The Impact of
      American Public Opinion on Foreign Policy. New
York: Macmillan, 1948.

355. Baldwin, David A. Economic Development and
      American Foreign Policy, 1943-62. Chicago: Uni-
versity of Chicago Press, 1966.

356. Barnet, Richard J. and Raskin, Marcus G. After
      20 Years: Alternatives to the Cold War in Europe.
New York: Random House, 1965.

357. _____. Intervention and Revolution: The United
      States in the Third World. New York: World, 1968.

358. _____. Roots of War. New York: Atheneum,
      1972.

359. Bartlett, Ruhl J. ed. The Record of American
      Diplomacy: Documents and Readings in the History of
American Foreign Relations. 4th ed. enl. New York:
Knopf, 1964.

360. Beal, John Robinson. John Foster Dulles. Rev. ed.
      New York: Harper, 1959. First published 1957.

361. Bell, Coral. Negotiation from Strength: A Study in
      the Politics of Power. New York: Knopf, 1963.

362. Biddle, Francis B. The World's Best Hope: A
      Discussion of the Role of the United States in the
Modern World. Chicago: University of Chicago Press,
1949.

363. Bloomfield, Lincoln P. The United Nations and U.S.
      Foreign Policy: A New Look at the National Interest.
Boston: Little, Brown, 1960.

364. Bohlen, Charles E. The Transformation of American
      Foreign Policy. New York: Norton, 1969.

365.   Bowie, Robert R. , "Analysis of Our Policy Machine,"
       New York Times Magazine, March 9, 1958, 16,
68-71.

366.   Bowles, Chester, "A Plea for Another Great Debate,"
       New York Times Magazine, February 28, 1954, 11, 24-6.

367.   _____. The Conscience of a Liberal: Selected
       Writings and Speeches.   Introd. and ed. by Henry
Steele Commager.   New York: Harper & Row, 1962.

368.   _____. Ideas, People and Peace.   New York:
       Harper, 1958.

369.   _____. New Dimensions of Peace.   New York:
       Harper, 1955.

370.   Brown, Seyom.   The Faces of Power: Constancy and
       Change in United States Foreign Policy from Truman
to Johnson.   New York: Columbia University Press, 1968.

371.   Burnham, James.   Containment or Liberation: An
       Inquiry into the Aims of United States Foreign Policy.
New York: Day, 1953.

372.   Byrnes, James F.   All in One Lifetime.   New York:
       Harper, 1958.

373.   _____. Speaking Frankly.   New York: Harper,
       1947.

374.   Capitanchik, David B.   The Eisenhower Presidency
       and American Foreign Policy.   London: Routledge
& Kegan Paul;   New York: Humanities Press, 1969.

375.   Carleton, William G.   The Revolution in American
       Foreign Policy: Its Global Range.   2d ed.   New
York: Random House, 1967.

376.   Challener, Richard D. and Fenton, John, "Which
       Way America?   Dulles Always Knew," American
Heritage, XXII (June, 1971), 12-13, 84-93.

377.   Chamberlin, William Henry.   Appeasement, Road to
       War.   New York: Rolton House, 1962.

378.   Cheever, Daniel S. and Haviland, H. Field.

American Foreign Policy and the Separation of
Powers. Cambridge: Harvard University Press, 1952.

379. Churchill, Winston S. The Second World War,
      Vol. VI, Triumph and Tragedy. Boston: Houghton
Mifflin, 1953.

380. Cleveland, Harlan, Mangone, Gerard J., and Adams,
      John Clarke. The Overseas Americans. New York:
McGraw-Hill, 1960.

381. Coffin, Tristram. Senator Fulbright: Portrait of a
      Public Philosopher. New York: Dutton, 1966.

382. Connally, Tom. My Name Is Tom Connally. By
      Tom Connally As Told to Alfred Steinberg. New
York: Crowell, 1954.

383. Cottrell, Leonard Slater and Eberhart, Sylvia.
      American Opinion on World Affairs in the Atomic
Age. Princeton: Princeton University Press, 1948.

384. Crabb, Cecil V. Bipartisan Foreign Policy: Myth or
      Reality? Evanston: Row, Peterson, 1957.

385. _____. The Elephants and the Grass: A Study in
      Nonalignment. New York: Praeger, 1965.

386. Curry, George. James F. Byrnes. New York:
      Cooper Square, 1965.

387. Dahl, Robert Alan. Congress and Foreign Policy.
      New York: Harcourt Brace, 1950.

388. Davis, Jerome and Hester, Hugh B. On the Brink.
      New York: Lyle Stuart, 1959.

389. Divine, Robert A. American Foreign Policy Since
      1945. Chicago: Quadrangle Books, 1969.

390. Documents on American Foreign Relations, Vol. VIII-
      [XXII] 1945/46-1960. 1945/46-1951 Boston: Pub-
lished for World Peace Foundation by Princeton University Press, 1948-1953; 1952-1960 New York: Published
for the Council on Foreign Relations by Harper, 1953-1961.
Supplement to v. VIII and IX is European Peace Treaties
after World War II ed. by Amelia C. Leiss.

391. Documents on International Affairs, 1947-1956. Lon-
      don: Issued under the Auspices of the Royal Institute
of International Affairs by the Oxford University Press,
1952-1959.

392. Donelan, Michael. The Ideas of American Foreign
      Policy. Philadelphia: Dufour Editions, 1965.

393. Drummond, Roscoe and Coblenz, Gastro. Duel at
      the Brink: John Foster Dulles' Command of American
Power. Garden City: Doubleday, 1960.

394. Dulles, Eleanor Lansing. American Foreign Policy
      in the Making. New York: Harper & Row, 1968.

395. _____. John Foster Dulles: The Last Year. New
      York: Harcourt, Brace and World, 1963.

396. Dulles, John Foster, "Challenge and Response in
      United States Foreign Policy," Foreign Affairs,
XXXVI (October, 1957), 25-43.

397. _____, "The Evolution of Foreign Policy," U. S.
      Department of State Bulletin, XXX (January 25, 1954),
107-110.

398. Elder, Robert Ellsworth. The Policy Machine: The
      Department of State and American Foreign Policy.
Syracuse: Syracuse University Press, 1960.

399. Elliott, William Yandell. United States Foreign
      Policy: Its Organization and Control. New York:
Columbia University Press, 1952.

400. Eubank, Keith. The Summit Conferences, 1919-1960.
      Norman: University of Oklahoma Press, 1966.

401. Farnsworth, David Nelson. The Senate Committee
      on Foreign Relations. Urbana: University of Illinois
Press, 1961. (Illinois Studies in the Social Sciences, v. 49).

402. Feis, Herbert. Foreign Aid and Foreign Policy.
      New York: St. Martin's Press, 1964.

403. Ferrell, Robert H. George C. Marshall. New York:
      Cooper Square Publishers, 1966. (American Secre-
taries of State and Their Diplomacy, Vol. XV).

404.   Finletter, Thomas K. Foreign Policy: The Next
        Phase, the 1960's. 2d ed. New York: Published
for the Council on Foreign Relations by Harper, 1960.
First published 1958.

405.   _____. Interim Report on the U.S. Search for a
        Substitute for Isolation. New York: Norton, 1968.

406.   _____. Power and Policy: U.S. Foreign Policy
        and Military Power in the Hydrogen Age. New York:
Harcourt, Brace, 1954.

407.   Fischer, John. Master Plan, U.S.A. : An Informal
        Report on America's Foreign Policy and the Men Who
Make It. New York: Harper, 1951.

408.   Freeland, Richard M. The Truman Doctrine and the
        Origins of McCarthyism: Foreign Policy, Domestic
Politics, and Internal Security, 1946-1948. New York:
Knopf, 1972.

409.   Fulbright, J. William. Fulbright of Arkansas: The
        Public Positions of a Private Thinker. Washington:
Luce, 1963.

410.   _____, "Reflections: In Thrall to Fear," New
        Yorker, XLVII (January 8, 1972), 41-62.

411.   Gallois, Pierre M. , "U.S. Foreign Policy: A Study
        in Military Strength and Diplomatic Weakness. "
Orbis, IX (Summer, 1965), 338-357.

412.   Gardner, Lloyd C. Architects of Illusion: Men and
        Ideas in American Foreign Policy, 1941-1949. Chi-
cago: Quadrangle Books, 1970.

413.   Gerson, Louis L. John Foster Dulles. New York:
        Cooper Square Publishers, 1967. (American Secre-
taries of State and Their Diplomacy, Vol. XVII).

414.   Goldwater, Barry M. Why Not Victory? A Fresh
        Look at American Foreign Policy. New York:
McGraw-Hill, 1962.

415.   Goold-Adams, Richard. John Foster Dulles: A
        Reappraisal. New York: Appleton-Century-Crofts,
1962.

416. Graber, Doris A. Crisis Diplomacy: A History of
     U.S. Intervention Policies and Practices. Washington:
Public Affairs Press, 1959.

417. _____. , "The Truman and Eisenhower Doctrines in
     the Light of the Doctrine of Non-Intervention," Poli-
tical Science Quarterly, LXXIII (September, 1958), 321-334.

418. Graebner, Norman A. The New Isolationism: A
     Study in Politics and Foreign Policy Since 1950.
New York: Ronald Press, 1956.

419. _____. , ed. An Uncertain Tradition: American
     Secretaries of State in the Twentieth Century. New
York: McGraw-Hill, 1961.

420. Guhin, Michael A. , "Dulles' Thoughts on International
     Politics: Myth and Reality," Orbis, XIII (Fall, 1969),
865-89.

421. Halle, Louis Joseph. Civilization and Foreign Policy:
     An Inquiry for Americans. New York: Harper, 1955.

422. Hammond, Paul Y. The Cold War Years: American
     Foreign Policy Since 1945. New York: Harcourt,
Brace and World, 1969.

423. Haviland, H. Field and others. The Formulation
     and Administration of United States Foreign Policy.
Washington: The Brookings Institution, 1960. "a report
for the Committee on Foreign Relations of the United States
Senate. " Also published by the Committee, Washington:
Government Printing Office, 1960.

424. Heller, Deane, and Heller, David. John Foster
     Dulles: Soldier for Peace. New York: Holt, Rine-
hart & Winston, 1960.

425. Hero, Alfred O. The Southerner and World Affairs.
     Baton Rouge: Louisiana State University Press, 1965.

426. Herz, John H. International Politics in the Atomic
     Age. New York: Columbia University Press, 1959.

427. Hoffmann, Stanley. Gulliver's Troubles: Or the
     Setting of American Foreign Policy. New York:
Published for the Council on Foreign Relations by McGraw-
Hill, 1968.

428.   Hoover, Herbert Clark.   Addresses upon the Ameri-
       can Road, 1945-1948. New York: Van Nostrand,
1949.

429.   _____.   Addresses upon the American Road, 1948-
       1950. Stanford: Stanford University Press, 1951.

430.   Horowitz, David, ed.   Containment and Revolution.
       Boston: Beacon Press, 1968.

431.   _____., ed.   Corporations and the Cold War.
       New York: Monthly Review Press, 1969.

432.   _____.   The Free World Colossus: A Critique of
       American Foreign Policy in the Cold War.   New
York: Hill and Wang, 1965.

433.   _____.   From Yalta to Vietnam: American Foreign
       Policy in the Cold War. Harmondsworth: Penguin,
1967.   Previously published as The Free World Colossus,
New York: Hill and Wang, 1965.

434.   Howe, Irving, ed.   A Dissenter's Guide to Foreign
       Policy. New York: Praeger, 1968.

435.   Hughes, Emmet John.   America the Vincible: A Brief
       Inquiry ... Dealing with Matters of Foreign Policy.
Garden City: Doubleday, 1959.

436.   Hughes, Henry Stuart.   An Approach to Peace and
       other Essays. New York: Atheneum, 1962.

437.   Jackson, Henry M.   Fact, Fiction and National
       Security. New York: Macfadden-Bartell, 1964.

438.   Jewell, Malcolm E.   Senatorial Politics & Foreign
       Policy. Lexington: University of Kentucky Press,
1962.

439.   Johnson, Haynes B. and Gwertzman, Bernard M.
       Fulbright: The Dissenter. New York: Doubleday,
1968.

440.   Kennan, George F.   American Diplomacy, 1900-1950.
       Chicago: University of Chicago Press, 1951.

441.   _____.   Memoirs, 1925-1950. Boston: Little,
       Brown, 1967.

442. _____. The Realities of American Foreign Policy.
     Princeton: Princeton University Press, 1954.

443. Kertesz, Stephen Denis, ed. American Diplomacy
     in a New Era. Notre Dame, Ind. , University of
Notre Dame Press, 1961.

444. Kirk, Grayson and others. The Changing Environ-
     ment of International Relations. Washington: Brook-
ings Institution, 1956.

445. Kissinger, Henry A. The Necessity for Choice:
     Prospects of American Foreign Policy. New York:
Harper, 1961.

446. _____. Nuclear Weapons and Foreign Policy.
     New York: Published for the Council on Foreign
Relations by Harper, 1957.

447. Kolko, Gabriel. The Roots of American Foreign
     Policy: An Analysis of Power and Purpose. Boston:
Beacon Press, 1969.

448. Kolko, Joyce and Kolko, Gabriel. The Limits of
     Power: The World and United States Foreign Policy,
1945-1954. New York: Harper & Row, 1972.

449. Landecker, Manfred. The President and Public
     Opinion: Leadership in Foreign Affairs. Washington:
Public Affairs Press, 1969.

450. Leacacos, John P. Fires in the In-Basket: The
     ABC's of the State Department. Cleveland: World,
1968.

451. Leahy, William D. I Was There: The Personal Story
     of the Chief of Staff to Presidents Roosevelt and
Truman. New York: McGraw-Hill, 1950.

452. Lens, Sidney. The Futile Crusade: Anti-Communism
     As American Credo. Chicago: Quadrangle Books,
1964.

453. Leopold, Richard W. The Growth of American
     Foreign Policy: A History. New York: Knopf, 1963.

454. Lerche, Charles O. The Uncertain South: Its

Changing Patterns of Politics in Foreign Policy.
Chicago: Quadrangle Books, 1964.

455. McCamy, James L. The Administration of American
      Foreign Affairs. New York: Knopf, 1950.

456. McCloy, John J. The Challenge to American Foreign
      Policy. Cambridge: Harvard University Press, 1953.

457. McInnis, Edgar Wardwell. The Atlantic Triangle and
      the Cold War. Toronto: Published for the Canadian
Institute of International Affairs by the University of Toronto
Press, 1959.

458. McNeill, William Hardy. America, Britain and
      Russia: Their Cooperation and Conflict, 1941-1946.
Oxford University Press, 1953. (Survey of International
Affairs, 1941-1946, Vol. III). Issued under the auspices
of the Royal Institute of International Affairs.

459. Magdoff, Harry. The Age of Imperialism: The
      Economics of U. S. Foreign Policy. New York:
Monthly Review Press, 1969.

460. Markel, Lester and others. Public Opinion and
      Foreign Policy. New York: Published for the Coun-
cil on Foreign Relations by Harper, 1949.

461. Marshall, Charles B. The Limits of Foreign Policy.
      New York: Holt, 1954.

462. Michigan. University. Survey Research Center.
      America's Role in World Affairs: Patterns of Citizen
Opinion, 1949-50. Ann Arbor: Survey Research Center,
Institute for Social Research, University of Michigan, 1952.

463. Millikan, Max F. and Rostow, Walt W. A Proposal:
      Key to an Effective Foreign Policy. New York:
Harper, 1957.

464. Mills, Charles Wright. The Causes of World War
      Three. New York: Simon and Schuster, 1958.

465. Molnar, Thomas Steven. The Two Faces of American
      Foreign Policy. Indianapolis: Bobbs-Merrill, 1962.

466. Morgenthau, Hans J. , "The Decline and Fall of

American Foreign Policy," New Republic, CXXXV (December 10, 1956), 11-16.

467. _____. Dilemmas of Politics. Chicago: University of Chicago Press, 1958.

468. _____. In Defense of the National Interest: A Critical Examination of American Foreign Policy. New York: Knopf, 1951.

469. _____. A New Foreign Policy for the United States. Published for the Council on Foreign Relations by Praeger, 1969.

470. _____. Politics among Nations: The Struggle for Power and Peace. 4th ed. New York: Knopf, 1967. First published 1948.

471. _____. Politics in the Twentieth Century. Chicago: University of Chicago Press, 1962. 3 vols. I. The Decline of Democratic Politics. II. The Impasse of American Foreign Policy. III. The Restoration of American Politics.

472. _____., "What the President and Mr. Dulles Don't Know," New Republic, CXXXV (December 17, 1956), 14-18. "The Decline and Fall of American Foreign Policy, II."

473. Murphy, Robert D. Diplomat among Warriors. Garden City: Doubleday, 1964.

474. Nieburg, Harold L. Nuclear Secrecy and Foreign Policy. Washington: Public Affairs Press, 1964.

475. Nixon, Richard M. The Challenges We Face. New York: McGraw-Hill, 1960.

476. Noble, G. Bernard. Christian A. Herter. New York: Cooper Square Publishers, 1970. (American Secretaries of State and Their Diplomacy, Vol. XVIII).

477. Osgood, Robert E. Alliances and American Foreign Policy. Baltimore: Johns Hopkins Press, 1968.

478. _____. and others. America and the World: From the Truman Doctrine to Vietnam. Baltimore, Johns

Hopkins Press, 1970.

479.   Parenti, Michael.   The Anti-Communist Impulse.
       New York: Random House, 1970.

480.   Perkins, Dexter.   The American Approach to Foreign
       Policy.   Rev. ed.   Cambridge: Harvard University
Press, 1952.

481.   _____.   The Diplomacy of a New Age: Major
       Issues in U.S. Policy Since 1945.   Bloomington:
Indiana University Press, 1967.

482.   Perlmutter, Oscar William, The Neo-Realism of
       Dean Acheson," Review of Politics, XXVI (January,
1964), 100-123.

483.   Price, Don Krasher, ed.   The Secretary of State.
       Englewood Cliffs, N. J.:   Prentice-Hall, 1960.

484.   Reitzel, William, Kaplan, Morton A., and Doblenz,
       Constance G., eds.   United States Foreign Policy,
1945-1955.   Washington: Brookings Institution, 1956.

485.   Robinson, James A.   Congress and Foreign Policy-
       Making: A Study in Legislative Influence and Initiative.
Rev. ed.   Homewood, Ill.:   Dorsey Press, 1967.

486.   Rosenau, James N.   National Leadership and Foreign
       Policy: A Case Study in the Mobilization of Public
Support.   Princeton: Princeton University Press, 1963.

487.   Rostow, Eugene V.   Law, Power, and the Pursuit of
       Peace.   Lincoln: University of Nebraska Press, 1968.

488.   Rostow, Walt W.   The View from the Seventh Floor.
       New York: Harper & Row, 1964.

489.   Rovere, Richard H., "The Interlocking Overlappers,"
       Progressive, XX (June, 1956), 33-35.

490.   Smith, Gaddis.   Dean Acheson.   New York: Cooper
       Square Publishers, 1972.   (American Secretaries of
State and Their Diplomacy, Vol. XVI).

491.   Snyder, Richard C., Bruck, H. W. and Sapin, Burton.
       Foreign Policy Decision Making: An Approach to the

Study of International Politics. New York: Free Press of Glencoe, 1962.

492. Spanier, John W. American Foreign Policy Since World War II. 3d rev. ed. New York: Praeger, 1968. First published 1961.

493. Steel, Ronald. Pax Americana. New York: Viking Press, 1967.

494. Stevenson, Adlai E. Call to Greatness. New York: Harper, 1954.

495. _____. An Ethic for Survival: Adlai Stevenson Speaks on International Affairs, 1936-1965. New York: Morrow, 1969.

496. _____. Putting First Things First: A Democratic View. New York: Random House, 1960.

497. Stillman, Edmund O. and Pfaff, William. The New Politics: America and the End of the Postwar World. New York: Coward McCann, 1961.

498. _____. _____. Power and Impotence: The Failure of America's Foreign Policy. New York: Random House, 1966.

499. Stromberg, Roland N. Collective Security and American Foreign Policy: From the League of Nations to NATO. New York: Praeger, 1963.

500. Sulzberger, Cyrus L. What's Wrong with U.S. Foreign Policy. New York: Harcourt, Brace, 1959.

501. Survey of International Affairs, 1947/1948 - 1955/ 1956. London: Issued under the Auspices of the Royal Institute of International Affairs by the Oxford University Press, 1952-1960. Supplemented by Documents on International Affairs. Supplement to Survey of International Affairs 1941-1946 is America, Britain and Russia by William Hardy McNeill.

502. Tugwell, Rexford G. A Chronicle of Jeopardy, 1945-55. Chicago: University of Chicago Press, 1955.

503. U.S. Congress. Senate. Committee on Foreign

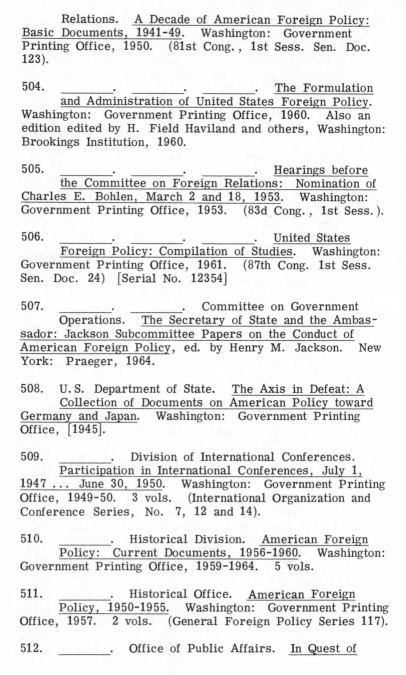

Relations. A Decade of American Foreign Policy:
Basic Documents, 1941-49. Washington: Government
Printing Office, 1950. (81st Cong. , 1st Sess. Sen. Doc.
123).

504. _____. _____. _____. The Formulation
and Administration of United States Foreign Policy.
Washington: Government Printing Office, 1960. Also an
edition edited by H. Field Haviland and others, Washington:
Brookings Institution, 1960.

505. _____. _____. _____. Hearings before
the Committee on Foreign Relations: Nomination of
Charles E. Bohlen, March 2 and 18, 1953. Washington:
Government Printing Office, 1953. (83d Cong. , 1st Sess.).

506. _____. _____. _____. United States
Foreign Policy: Compilation of Studies. Washington:
Government Printing Office, 1961. (87th Cong. 1st Sess.
Sen. Doc. 24) [Serial No. 12354]

507. _____. _____. Committee on Government
Operations. The Secretary of State and the Ambas-
sador: Jackson Subcommittee Papers on the Conduct of
American Foreign Policy, ed. by Henry M. Jackson. New
York: Praeger, 1964.

508. U. S. Department of State. The Axis in Defeat: A
Collection of Documents on American Policy toward
Germany and Japan. Washington: Government Printing
Office, [1945].

509. _____. Division of International Conferences.
Participation in International Conferences, July 1,
1947 ... June 30, 1950. Washington: Government Printing
Office, 1949-50. 3 vols. (International Organization and
Conference Series, No. 7, 12 and 14).

510. _____. Historical Division. American Foreign
Policy: Current Documents, 1956-1960. Washington:
Government Printing Office, 1959-1964. 5 vols.

511. _____. Historical Office. American Foreign
Policy, 1950-1955. Washington: Government Printing
Office, 1957. 2 vols. (General Foreign Policy Series 117).

512. _____. Office of Public Affairs. In Quest of

Peace and Security: Selected Documents on American Foreign Policy, 1941-1951. Washington: Government Printing Office, 1951. (General Foreign Policy Series 53).

513. The United States in World Affairs, 1945/47-1960. New York: Published for the Council on Foreign Relations by Harper, 1947-1961.

514. Vagts, Alfred. Defense and Diplomacy: The Soldier and the Conduct of Foreign Relations. New York: King's Crown Press, 1956.

515. Van Alstyne, Richard W. American Crisis Diplomacy: The Quest for Collective Security 1918-1952. Stanford: Stanford University Press, 1952.

516. Vandenberg, Arthur H. The Private Papers of Senator Vandenberg, ed. by Arthur H. Vandenberg, Jr. and Joe Alexis Morris. Boston: Houghton Mifflin, 1952.

517. Venkataramani, M. S. Undercurrents in American Foreign Relations: Four Studies. New York: Asia Publishing House, 1965.

518. Walker, Richard L. "E. R. Stettinius, Jr." In American Secretaries of State and Their Diplomacy, ed. by Robert Ferrell, Vol. XIV, pp. 1-83, 318-340, 397-404. New York: Cooper Square Publishers, 1965.

519. Warburg, James P. Agenda for Action: Toward Peace through Disengagement. New York: Academy Books, 1957.

520. _____. Last Call for Common Sense. New York: Harcourt Brace, 1949.

521. _____. The United States in the Postwar World: What We Have Done, What We Have Left Undone, and What We Can and Must Do. New York: Atheneum, 1966.

522. Welles, Sumner. Where Are We Heading? New York: Harper, 1946.

523. Westerfield, H. Bradford. Foreign Policy and Party Politics: Pearl Harbor to Korea. New Haven: Yale University Press.

524. _____. The Instruments of America's Foreign
       Policy. New York: Crowell, 1963.

525. Whelan, Joseph G. , "George Kennan and His Influence
       on American Foreign Policy," Virginia Quarterly
Review, XXXV (Spring, 1959), 196-220.

526. Wilbur, William H.   Guideposts for the Future: A
       New American Foreign Policy. Chicago: Regnery,
1954.

527. Williams, William Appleman.   The Tragedy of
       American Diplomacy. Rev. and enl ed.   New York:
Dell, 1962.

528. Woodrow Wilson Foundation.   The Political Economy
       of American Foreign Policy: Its Concepts, Strategy
and Limits.   Report of a Study Group Sponsored by the
Woodrow Wilson Foundation and the National Planning Association.   New York: Holt, 1955.

529. _____. United States Foreign Policy: Its Organi-
       zation and Control.   Report of a Study Group for the
Woodrow Wilson Foundation.   New York: Columbia University Press, 1952.

530. Wright, Quincy, ed.   A Foreign Policy for the United
       States.   Chicago: University of Chicago Press, 1947.

531. Zimmern, Sir Alfred Eckhard.   The American Road
       to World Peace. New York: Dutton, 1953.

B.   RELATIONS WITH PARTICULAR AREAS

1. Africa

532. American Assembly.   The United States and Africa,
       ed. by Walter Goldschmidt.   Rev. ed.   New York:
Published for the American Assembly by Praeger, 1963.
Completely revised.

533. Bowles, Chester.   Africa's Challenge to America.
       Berkeley: University of California Press, 1956.

2. Asia

a. China

534. The Amerasia Papers: A Clue to the Catastrophe of
       China. Washington: Government Printing Office,
1970. (91st Cong. , 1st Sess.) 2 vols. Introduction by
Anthony Kubek. Prepared by the Subcommittee to Investi-
gate the Administration of the Internal Security Act and
Other Internal Security Laws. ...

535. American Assembly. The United States and the Far
       East. 2d ed. Englewood Cliffs, N. J. , Prentice-
Hall, 1962. First published 1956.

536. Appleton, Sheldon. The Eternal Triangle? Com-
       munist China, the United States and the United
Nations. East Lansing: Michigan State University Press,
1961.

537. Barnett, A. Doak. Communist China and Asia,
       Challenge to American Foreign Policy. New York:
Published for the Council on Foreign Relations by Harper,
1960.

538. Bate, Henry Maclear. Report from Formosa. New
       York: Dutton, 1952.

539. Beal, John Robinson. Marshall in China. Garden
       City: Doubleday, 1970.

540. Blum, Robert. The United States and China in
       World Affairs. New York: Published for the Coun-
cil on Foreign Relations by McGraw-Hill, 1966.

541. Bullitt, William C. , "Report to the American People
       on China," Life, XXIII (October 13, 1947), 35-37,
139-154.

542. Campbell, Alexander. Unbind Your Sons: The Cap-
       tivity of America in Asia. New York: Liveright,
1970.

543. Chang, Hsin-Hai. America and China: A New Ap-
       proach to Asia. New York: Simon & Schuster, 1966.

544. Clubb, Oliver E. The United States and the

Sino-Soviet Bloc in Southeast Asia. Washington:
Brookings Institution, 1962.

545.   Cohen, Warren I. America's Response to China: An
       Interpretative History of Sino-American Relations.
New York: Wiley, 1971.

546.   Congressional Quarterly Service. China and U.S.
       Far East Policy, 1945-1966. Washington: Congres-
sional Quarterly Service, 1966.

547.   DeJaegher, Raymond J. and Kuhn, Irene C. The
       Enemy Within: An Eyewitness Account of the Com-
munist Conquest of China. Garden City: Doubleday, 1952.

548.   Dulles, Foster Rhea. American Policy toward
       Communist China, 1949-1969. New York: Crowell,
1972.

549.   Fairbank, John K. China: The People's Middle
       Kingdom and the U.S.A. Cambridge: Belknap Press
of Harvard University Press, 1967.

550.   _____. The United States and China. 3d ed.
       Cambridge: Harvard University Press, 1971.

551.   Feis, Herbert. The China Tangle: The American
       Effort in China from Pearl Harbor to the Marshall
Mission. Princeton: Princeton University Press, 1953.
Reprinted New York: Atheneum, 1965.

552.   Flynn, John T. The Lattimore Story. New York:
       Devin-Adair, 1953.

553.   Guhin, Michael A., "The United States and the
       Chinese People's Republic: The Non-Recognition Policy
Reviewed," International Affairs (London) XLV, (January,
1969), 44-63.

554.   Iriye, Akira, ed. U.S. Policy toward China: Testi-
       mony Taken from the Senate Foreign Relations Com-
mittee Hearings, 1966. Boston: Little, Brown, 1968.

555.   Keeley, Joseph Charles. The China Lobby Man: The
       Story of Alfred Kohlberg. New Rochelle, N.Y.:
Arlington House, 1969.

556.   Kerr, George H.   Formosa Betrayed.   Boston:
       Houghton Mifflin, 1965.

557.   Koen, Ross Y.   The China Lobby in American
       Politics.   New York: Macmillan, 1960.

558.   Kubek, Anthony.   How the Far East Was Lost:
       American Policy and the Creation of Communist
China, 1941-1949.   Chicago: Regnery, 1963.

559.   Latourette, Kenneth Scott.   The American Record in
       the Far East, 1945-1951.   New York: Macmillan,
1952.

560.   Melby, John F. , "The Origins of the Cold War in
       China," Pacific Affairs, XLI (Spring, 1968), 19-33.

561.   North, Robert C.   Moscow and the Chinese Commu-
       nists.   2d ed.   Stanford: Stanford University Press,
1963.

562.   Rankin, Karl Lott.   China Assignment.   Seattle:
       University of Washington Press, 1964.

563.   Service, John S.   The Amerasia Papers: Some
       Problems in the History of U. S.-China Relations.
Berkeley: University of California Center for Chinese
Studies, 1971.   (China Research Monograph 7).

564.   Steele, Archibald T.   The American People and
       China.   New York: Published for the Council on
Foreign Relations by McGraw-Hill, 1966.

565.   Stilwell, Joseph W.   The Stilwell Papers.   Ed. by
       Theodore White.   New York: Sloane, 1948.

566.   Strausz-Hupé, Robert, Cottrell, Alvin J. and
       Dougherty, James E.   American-Asian Tensions.
New York: Praeger, 1956.

567.   Terrill, Ross, "When America 'Lost' China: The
       Case of John Carter Vincent," Atlantic, CCXXIV
(November, 1969), 78-86.

568.   Tsou, Tang.   America's Failure in China, 1941-50.
       Chicago: University of Chicago Press, 1963.

569. Tuchman, Barbara W. Stilwell and the American
      Experience in China, 1911-45. New York:
Macmillan, 1971.

570. U. S. Congress. Senate. Committee on Foreign
      Relations. China, Vietnam and the United States:
Highlights of the Hearings. Washington: Public Affairs
Press, 1966.

571. _____. _____. _____. U. S. Policy with
      Respect to Mainland China, Hearings. Washington:
Government Printing Office, 1966. (89th Cong. , 2d Sess. ,
March 8-30, 1966).

572. U. S. Department of State. The China White Paper,
      August 1949. Stanford: Stanford University Press,
1967. Originally issued as United States Relations with
China. Reissued with a new introduction by Lyman P.
Van Slyke.

573. _____. United States Relations with China.
      Washington: Government Printing Office, 1949.
(Far Eastern Series 30).

574. Utley, Freda. The China Story. Chicago: Regnery,
      1951.

575. Vinacke, Harold Monk. The United States and the
      Far East, 1945-1951. New York: American Institute
of Pacific Relations, 1952.

576. Wang, Tao. America Bewildered. New York:
      Philosophical Library, 1965.

577. Wedemeyer, Albert C. Wedemeyer Reports! New
      York: Holt, 1958.

578. Young, Kenneth T. Negotiating with the Chinese
      Communists: The United States Experience, 1953-
1967. New York: Published for the Council on Foreign
Relations by McGraw-Hill, 1968.

    b.   India

579. Bowles, Chester. Ambassador's Report. New York:
      Harper, 1954.

580. Brown, William Norman. The United States and
      India and Pakistan. Rev. and enl. ed. Cambridge:
Harvard University Press, 1963.

581. Rosinger, Lawrence K. India and the United States:
      Political and Economic Relations. New York: Pub-
lished for the American Institute of Pacific Relations by
Macmillan, 1950.

      c. Japan

582. Brown, Delmer M. Nationalism in Japan: An Intro-
      ductory Historical Analysis. Berkeley: University of
California Press, 1955.

583. Cohen, Bernard Cecil. The Political Process and
      Foreign Policy: The Making of the Japanese Peace
Settlement. Princeton: Princeton University Press, 1957.

584. Cohen, Jerome B. Japan's Economy in War and
      Reconstruction. Minneapolis: University of Minnesota
Press, 1949.

585. Colbert, Evelyn S. The Left Wing in Japanese
      Politics. New York: Institute of Pacific Relations,
1952.

586. Dunn, Frederick S. and others. Peace-Making and
      the Settlement with Japan, by Frederick S. Dunn,
Annemarie Shimony, Percy E. Corbett and Bernard C.
Cohen, Princeton: Princeton University Press, 1963.

587. Fearey, Robert. The Occupation of Japan--Second
      Phase, 1948-1950. New York: Macmillan, 1950.

588. Feis, Herbert. Contest over Japan. New York:
      Norton, 1967.

589. Gunther, John. The Riddle of MacArthur: Japan,
      Korea, and the Far East. New York: Harper, 1951.

590. Hadley, Eleanor M. Antitrust in Japan. Princeton:
      Princeton University Press, 1970.

591. Hunt, Frazier. The Untold Story of Douglas
      MacArthur. New York: Devin-Adair, 1954.

52   The Truman/Eisenhower Years

592.   Ike, Nobutaka.   The Beginnings of Political Democ-
       racy in Japan.   Baltimore: Johns Hopkins University
Press, 1950.

593.   Kase, Toshikazu.   Journey to the Missouri.   New
       Haven: Yale University Press, 1950.

594.   Lee, Clark Gould and Henschel, Richard.   Douglas
       MacArthur.   New York: Holt, 1952.

595.   MacArthur, Douglas.   Reminiscences.   New York:
       McGraw-Hill, 1964.

596.   _____.   Representative Speeches of General of the
       Army Douglas MacArthur, comp. by the Legislative
Reference Service, Library of Congress.   Washington:
Government Printing Office, 1964.   (88th Cong. , 2d Sess.
Senate Doc. No. 95) [Serial No. 12622].

597.   _____.   A Soldier Speaks: Public Papers and
       Speeches of General of the Army, Douglas MacArthur.
New York: Praeger, 1965.

598.   Martin, Edwin M.   The Allied Occupation of Japan.
       Stanford: Stanford University Press, 1948.

599.   Packard, George R.   Protest in Tokyo: The Security Treaty
       Crisis of 1960.   Princeton: Princeton Univ. Press, 1966.

600.   Reischauer, Edwin O.   The United States and Japan.
       3d ed.   Cambridge: Harvard University Press, 1965.

601.   Sebald, William J. and Brines, Russell.   With
       MacArthur in Japan: A Personal History of the
Occupation.   New York: Norton, 1965.

602.   Supreme Command for the Allied Powers.   Report
       of General MacArthur, Prepared by His General
Staff.   Washington: Government Printing Office, 1966.
2 vols. in 4.   Vol. I Supplement, MacArthur in Japan.

603.   Swearingen, Rodger and Langer, Paul.   Red Flag in
       Japan: International Communism in Action, 1919-
1951.   Cambridge: Harvard University Press, 1952.

604.   Toland, John.   The Rising Sun: The Decline and Fall
       of the Japanese Empire, 1936-1945.   New York:

Random House, 1970.   2 vols.

605.   U. S. Department of State.   The Axis in Defeat: A
        Collection of Documents on American Policy toward
Germany and Japan.   Washington: Government Printing
Office, 1945.

606.   Weinstein, Martin E.   Japan's Postwar Defense
        Policy, 1947-1968.   New York: Columbia University
Press, 1971.   (Studies of the East Asian Institute of
Columbia University).

607.   Whitney, Courtney.   MacArthur: His Rendezvous with
        History.   New York: Knopf, 1956.

608.   Willoughby, Charles A. and Chamberlain, John.
        MacArthur, 1941-1951.   New York: McGraw-Hill,
1954.

       d.   The Philippines

609.   Grunder, Garel A. and Livezey, William E.   The
        Philippines and the United States.   Norman: Univer-
sity of Oklahoma Press, 1951.

610.   Taylor, George E.   The Philippines and the United
        States: Problems of Partnership.   New York: Pub-
lished for the Council on Foreign Relations by Praeger,
1964.

       e.   Southeast Asia

611.   Fall, Bernard B. and Smith, Roger, eds.   Anatomy
        of a Crisis: The Laotian Crisis of 1960-1961.   Gar-
den City: Doubleday, 1969.

612.   Shaplen, Robert.   Time Out of Hand: Revolution and
        Reaction in Southeast Asia.   New York: Harper &
Row, 1969.

       f.   Vietnam

613.   Bator, Victor.   Vietnam: A Diplomatic Tragedy: The
        Origins of the United States Involvement.   Dobbs
Ferry, N. Y. , Oceana Publications, 1965.

614.   Buttinger, Joseph.   Vietnam: A Dragon Embattled.

New York: Praeger, 1967. 2 vols. Vol. I, From
Colonialism to the Vietminh. Vol. II, Vietnam at War.

615.   Cameron, Allan W. , ed.   Vietnam Crisis: A Docu-
       mentary History.   Ithaca: Cornell University Press,
1971.   Vol. I, 1940-1956.

616.   Cooper, Chester L.   The Lost Crusade: America
       in Vietnam.   New York: Dodd, Mead, 1970.

617.   Devillers, Philippe and Lacouture, Jean.   End of a
       War: Indochina, 1954.   New York: Praeger, 1969.

618.   Drachman, Edward R.   United States Policy toward
       Vietnam, 1940-1945.   Rutherford, N. J. :   Fairleigh
Dickinson University Press, 1970.

619.   Falk, Richard A. , ed.   The Vietnam War and Inter-
       national Law.   Princeton: Princeton University Press,
1968-1969.   2 vols.

620.   Fall, Bernard B.   Hell in a Very Small Place: The
       Siege of Dien Bien Phu.   Philadelphia: Lippincott,
1967.

621.   _____.   Street without Joy.   4th ed.   Harrisburg:
       Stackpole, 1964.

622.   _____.   Two Vietnams: A Political and Military
       Analysis.   Rev. ed.   New York: Praeger, 1964.

623.   _____.   The Viet-Minh Regime: Government and
       Administration in the Democratic Republic of Vietnam.
Rev. and enl. ed.   New York: Institute of Pacific Rela-
tions, 1956.   Issued jointly with the Southeast Asia Program,
Cornell University.

624.   _____.   Viet-Nam Witness, 1953-66.   New York:
       Praeger, 1966.

625.   Goodwin, Richard N.   Triumph or Tragedy: Reflections
       on Vietnam.   New York: Random House, 1966.

626.   Gruening, Ernest and Beaser, Herbert Wilson.
       Vietnam Folly.   Washington: National Press, 1968.

627.   Gurtov, Melvin.   The First Vietnam Crisis: Chinese

Communist Strategy and United States Involvement,
1953-54. New York: Columbia University Press, 1967.

628.   Hammer, Ellen Joy.   The Struggle for Indochina,
       1940-1955.   Stanford: Stanford University Press,
1966c1955.

629.   _____.   The Struggle for Indochina Continues:
       Geneva to Bandung.   Stanford: Stanford University
Press,   1955.

630.   Hull, Roger H. and Novogrod, John C.   Law and
       Vietnam.   Dobbs Ferry, N. Y. ,   Oceana Publications,
1968.

631.   Kahin, George M. and Lewis, John W.   The United
       States in Vietnam.   Rev. ed.   New York: Dial
Press,   1967 i. e. 1969.

632.   Lacouture, Jean.   Vietnam: Between Two Truces.
New York: Random House,   1966.

633.   Montgomery, John D.   The Politics of Foreign Aid:
       American Experience in Southeast Asia.   New York:
Published for the Council on Foreign Relations by Praeger,
1962.

634.   The Pentagon Papers As Published by the New York
       Times.   Based on Investigative Reporting by Neil
Sheehan, Hedrick Smith, E. W. Kenworthy and Fox Butterfield.   New York: Bantam Books,   1971.

635.   The Pentagon Papers As Published by the New York
       Times.   The Pentagon History Was Obtained by Neil
Sheehan.   Written by Neil Sheehan [and others].   New
York: Quadrangle Books,   1971.

636.   The Pentagon Papers: The Defense Department His-
       tory of the United States Decision Making on Vietnam.
The Senator Gravel Edition.   Boston: Beacon Press,   1971.
4 vols.

637.   Randle, Robert F.   Geneva, 1954: The Settlement of
       the Indochinese War.   Princeton: Princeton Univer-
sity Press,   1969.

638.   Schoenbrun, David.   Vietnam: How We Got In: How

to Get Out. New York: Atheneum Publishers, 1968.

639. Shaplen, Robert. The Lost Revolution: The Story of
      Twenty Years of Neglected Opportunities in Vietnam
and of America's Failure to Foster Democracy There.
New York: Harper & Row, 1965.

640. Taylor, Telford. Nuremberg and Vietnam: An
      American Tragedy. Chicago: Quadrangle Books,
distributed by Random House, 1970.

641. U.S. Congress. Senate. Committee on Foreign
      Relations. Background Information Relating to South-
east Asia and Vietnam. 3d rev. ed. Washington: Government Printing Office, 1967.

642. _____. _____. _____. China, Vietnam
      and the United States: Highlights of the Hearings ...
Washington: Public Affairs Press, 1966.

643. _____. _____. _____. The Vietnam
      Hearings. New York: Random House, 1966.

644. U.S. Department of Defense. United States-Vietnam
      Relations, 1945-1967. Study Prepared by the Depart-
ment of Defense, Printed for the Use of the House Committee on Armed Services. Washington: Government Printing Office, 1971. 12 vols.

645. Warner, Geoffrey, "Escalation in Vietnam, the Pre-
      cedents of 1954," International Affairs, XLI (April,
1965), 266-277.

3. Latin America and Canada

646. Adams, Richard N. and others. Social Change in
      Latin America Today: Its Implications for United
States Policy. New York: Published for the Council on
Foreign Relations by Harper, 1960.

647. Alexander, Robert J. Communism in Latin America.
      New Brunswick, N. J.: Rutgers University Press,
1957.

648. Cabot, John M. Toward Our Common American
      Destiny. Medford, Mass.: Fletcher School of Law
and Diplomacy, 1955.

649.   Eisenhower, Milton S.   The Wine Is Bitter: The
        United States and Latin America.   Garden City:
Doubleday, 1963.

650.   Green, David.   The Containment of Latin America:
        A History of the Myths and Realities of the Good
Neighbor Policy.   Chicago: Quadrangle Books, 1971.

651.   Lazo, Mario.   Dagger in the Heart: American Policy
        Failures in Cuba.   New York: Funk & Wagnalls,
1968.

652.   Lieuwen, Edwin.   Arms and Politics in Latin
        America.   Rev. ed.   New York: Published for the
Council on Foreign Relations by Praeger, 1960.

653.   Mecham, John Lloyd.   The United States and Inter-
        American Security, 1889-1960.   Austin: University
of Texas Press, 1961.

654.   Palmer, Thomas W.   Search for a Latin American
        Policy.   Gainesville: University of Florida Press,
1957.

655.   Pflaum, Irving Peter.   Tragic Island: How Com-
        munism Came to Cuba.   Englewood Cliffs, N. J. :
Prentice-Hall, 1961.

656.   Rivero, Nicolas.   Castro's Cuba: An American
        Dilemma.   Washington: Luce, 1962.

657.   Rubottom, Roy R. , "Basic Principles Governing
        United States Relations with Latin America," United
States Department of State Bulletin, XXXVIII (April 14,
1958), 608-614.

658.   Slater, Jerome.   The OAS and United States Foreign
        Policy.   Columbus: Ohio State University Press,
1967.

659.   Smith, Earl E. T.   The Fourth Floor: An Account
        of the Castro Communist Revolution.   New York:
Random House, 1963.

660.   Soward, F. H. , "The Changing Relations of Canada
        and the United States Since the Second World War,"
Pacific Historical Review, XXII (May, 1953), 155-168.

661.   U. S. Congress. House. Committee on Appropria-
       tions. A Review of United States Government Opera-
tions in Latin America, 1958, by Allen J. Ellender.
Washington: Government Printing Office, 1959. (86th
Cong. , 1st Sess, House Document 13).

662.   Wagner, R. Harrison. United States Policy toward
       Latin America: A Study in Domestic and International
Politics. Stanford: Stanford University Press, 1970.

663.   Whitaker, Arthur P. Argentine Upheaval: Peron's
       Fall and the New Regime. New York: Praeger,
1956. (Foreign Policy Research Institute Series no. 1).

664.   _____. The United States and Argentina. Cam-
       bridge: Harvard University Press, 1954.

665.   Williams, William Appleman. The United States,
       Cuba, and Castro: An Essay on the Dynamics of
Revolution and the Dissolution of Empire. New York:
Monthly Review Press, 1962.

666.   Zeitlin, Maurice and Scheer, Robert. Cuba, Tragedy
       in Our Hemisphere. New York: Grove Press, 1963.

4.   Middle East

     a.   General

667.   Bickerton, Ian J. , "President Truman's Recognition
       of Israel," American Jewish Historical Quarterly,
LVIII (December, 1968), 173-240.

668.   Campbell, John C. Defense of the Middle East:
       Problems of American Policy. 2nd ed. New York:
Published for the Council on Foreign Relations by Harper,
1960.

669.   Crossman, Richard H. S. Palestine Mission: A
       Personal Record. New York: Harper, 1947.

670.   Crum, Bartley C. Behind the Silken Curtain: A
       Personal Account of Anglo-American Diplomacy in
Palestine and the Middle East. New York: Simon &
Schuster, 1947.

671.   Dunner, Joseph. Democratic Bulwark in the Middle

East: A Review of Israel's Social, Economic, and
Political Problems ... from 1948 to 1953.   Grinnell, Ia. ,
Grinnell College Press, 1953.

672. _____. The Republic of Israel: Its History and
       Its Promise. New York: McGraw-Hill, 1950.

673. Ellis, Harry B. Challenge in the Middle East:
       Communist Influence and American Policy. New
York: Ronald Press, 1960.

674. Feis, Herbert. The Birth of Israel: The Tousled
       Diplomatic Bed. New York: Norton, 1969.

675. Halperin, Samuel. The Political World of American
       Zionism. Detroit, Wayne State University Press,
1961.

676. Leeman, Wayne A. The Price of Middle East Oil:
       An Essay in Political Economy. Ithaca: Cornell
University Press, 1962.

677. Lilienthal, Alfred M. The Other Side of the Coin:
       An American Perspective of the Arab-Israeli Conflict.
New York: Devin-Adair, 1965.

678. _____. There Goes the Middle East. New York:
       Devin-Adair 1957. 3d ed. New York: Bookmailer,
1960.

679. _____. What Price Israel? Chicago: Regnery,
       1953.

680. Mehdi, Mohammad T. Of Lions, Chained: An Arab
       Looks at America. San Francisco: New World
Press, 1962.

681. Mikesell, Raymond F. and Chenery, Hollis B.
       Arabian Oil: America's Stake in the Middle East.
Chapel Hill: University of North Carolina Press, 1949.

682. Safran, Nadav. The United States and Israel. Cam-
       bridge: Harvard University Press, 1963.

683. Thomas, Lewis V. and Frye, Richard N. The
       United States and Turkey and Iran. Cambridge:
Harvard University Press, 1951.

684.   Thornburg, Max W.   People and Policy in the Middle
       East: A Study of Social Political Change As a Basis
for United States Policy.   New York: Norton, 1964.

685.   U. S. Department of State.   United States Policy in
       the Middle East, September 1956-June 1957, Docu-
ments.   Washington: Government Printing Office, 1957.

   b.   The Suez Expedition

686.   Beaufre, André.   The Suez Expedition, 1956.   Tr.
       from the French by Richard Barry.   New York:
Praeger, 1969.

687.   Eden, Anthony.   Full Circle.   Boston: Houghton
       Mifflin, 1960.   Eden's Memoirs.

688.   Farnie, D. A.   East and West of Suez: The Suez
       Canal in History 1854-1956.

689.   Finer, Herman.   Dulles over Suez: The Theory and
       Practice of His Diplomacy.   Chicago: Quadrangle
Books, 1964.

690.   Love, Kenneth.   Suez, the Twice-Fought War: A
       History.   New York: McGraw-Hill, 1969.

691.   Neustadt, Richard E.   Alliance Politics.   New York:
       Columbia University Press, 1970.

692.   Thomas, Hugh.   Suez.   New York: Harper & Row,
       1967.   English title: The Suez Affair.

693.   U. S. Department of State.   The Suez Canal Problem,
       July 26-September 22, 1956.   Washington: Govern-
ment Printing Office, 1956.   (International Organization and
Conference Series II).

5.   Russia

   a.   General

694.   Bouscaren, Anthony T.   Soviet Foreign Policy: A
       Pattern of Persistence.   New York: Fordham Uni-
versity Press, 1962.

695.   Byrnes, James F. , "Byrnes Answers Truman,"

Collier's, CXXIX (April 26, 1952), 15-17+.

696. Clark, Mark Wayne. Calculated Risk. New York: Harper, 1950.

697. Deutscher, Isaac. The Great Contest: Russia and the West. New York: Oxford University Press, 1960.

698. _____. Russia: What Next? New York: Oxford University Press, 1953.

699. _____. Stalin: A Political Biography. 2nd ed. New York: Oxford University Press, 1967.

700. Druks, Herbert. Harry S. Truman and the Russians, 1945-1953. New York: Robert Speller, 1967.

701. Harriman, W. Averell. America and Russia in a Changing World: A Half Century of Personal Observations. Garden City: Doubleday, 1971.

702. _____. Peace with Russia? New York: Simon & Schuster, 1959.

703. Margold, Stella K. Let's Do Business with Russia: Why We Should and How We Can. New York: Harper, 1948.

704. Mosely, Philip E. The Kremlin and World Politics: Studies in Soviet Policy and Action. New York: Vintage Books, 1960.

705. _____., ed. "The Soviet Union Since World War II," American Academy of Political and Social Science. Annals, CCLXIII (May, 1949), 1-211.

706. Plischke, Elmer, "Eisenhower's Correspondence Diplomacy with the Kremlin--Case Study in Soviet Diplomatics, Journal of Politics, XXX (February, 1968), 137-159.

707. Rostow, Walt W., Levin, Arnold, and others. Dynamics of Soviet Society. New York: Norton, 1952.

708. Stalin, Joseph. Correspondence [between Stalin, Roosevelt and Churchill]. Moscow: Foreign

Languages Publishing House, 1957. 2 vols. in 1.

709. _____. Correspondence with Churchill, Attlee,
       Roosevelt and Truman, 1941-1945. New York:
Dutton, 1958.

710. Stevenson, Adlai E. Friends and Enemies: What I
       Learned in Russia. New York: Harper, 1959.

711. Stoessinger, John G. and McKelvey, Robert G. The
       United Nations and the Superpowers: United States-
Soviet Interaction at the United Nations. 2d ed. New York:
Random House, 1970.

712. Tompkins, Pauline. American-Russian Relations in
       the Far East. New York: Macmillan, 1949.

713. Ulam, Adam B. Expansion and Coexistence: The
       History of Soviet Foreign Policy, 1917-1967. New
York: Praeger, 1968.

714. U. S. Department of Defense. The Entry of the
       Soviet Union into the War against Japan: Military
Plans, 1941-1945. Washington: Department of Defense,
1955.

715. Warburg, James P. How to Co-Exist without Playing
       the Kremlin's Game. Boston: Beacon Press, 1952.

716. Warth, Robert D. Soviet Russia in World Politics.
       New York: Twayne Publishers, 1963.

717. Welch, William. American Images of Soviet Foreign
       Policy: An Inquiry into Recent Appraisals from the
Academic Community. New Haven: Yale University Press,
1970.

718. Wolfe, Bertram D. , "Communist Ideology and Soviet
       Foreign Policy," Foreign Affairs, XLI (October,
1962), 152-170.

   b. The U-2 Incident

719. McCamy, James L. The Conduct of the New
       Diplomacy. New York: Harper & Row, 1964.

720. Powers, Francis Gary and Gentry, Curt. Operation

Overflight: The U-2 Spy Pilot Tells His Story for the First Time. New York: Holt, Rinehart & Winston, 1970.

721. _____, defendant. The Trial of the U2: Exclusive Authorized Account of the Court Proceedings of the Case. Heard before the Military Division of the Supreme Court of the U. S. S. R. , Moscow August 17, 18, 19, 1960. Chicago: Translation World Publishers, 1960.

722. Wise, David and Ross, Thomas B. The U-2 Affair. New York: Random House, 1962.

6. Western Europe

723. Ambrose, Stephen E. Eisenhower and Berlin, 1945: The Decision to Halt at the Elbe. New York: Norton, 1967.

724. Beugel, Ernst Hans van der. From Marshall Aid to Atlantic Partnership: European Integration As a Concern of American Foreign Policy. New York: Elsevier Publishing Company, 1966.

725. Brinton, Crane. The Americans and the French. Cambridge: Harvard University Press, 1968.

726. Dulles, Eleanor Lansing. One Germany or Two: The Struggle at the Heart of Europe. Stanford: Hoover Institution Press, Stanford University, 1970.

727. Epstein, Leon D. Britain--Uneasy Ally. Chicago: University of Chicago Press, 1954.

728. Friedmann, Wolfgang Gaston. The Allied Military Government of Germany. Published under the auspices of the London Institute of World Affairs, London: Stevens & Sons, 1947.

729. Gelber, Lionel M. America in Britain's Place: The Leadership of the West and Anglo-American Unity. New York: Praeger, 1961.

730. _____. Reprieve from War: A Manual for Realists. New York: Macmillan, 1950.

731. Golay, John F. The Founding of the Federal Republic of Germany. Chicago: University of Chicago Press, 1958.

732.   Hartmann, Frederick H.   Germany between East and
        West: The Reunification Problem.   Englewood Cliffs,
N. J.;   Prentic-Hall, 1965.

733.   Holborn, Hajo.   American Military Government: Its
        Organization and Policies.   Washington: Infantry
Journal Press, 1947.

734.   Kousoulas, Dimitrios George.   Revolution and Defeat:
        The Story of the Greek Communist Party.   New York:
Oxford University Press, 1965.

735.   Litchfield, Edward H. and associates.   Governing
        Postwar Germany.   Ithaca: Cornell University Press,
1953.

736.   McNeill, William Hardy.   Greece: American Aid in
        Action, 1947-1956.   New York: Twentieth Century
Fund, 1957.

737.   Merkl, Peter H.   The Origin of the West-German
        Republic.   New York: Oxford University Press, 1963.

738.   Middleton, Drew.   The Struggle for Germany.
        Indianapolis: Bobbs-Merrill, 1949.

739.   Mosely, Philip E., "Dismemberment of Germany:
        The Allied Negotiations from Yalta to Potsdam,"
Foreign Affairs, XXVIII (April, 1950), 497-498.

740.   _____., "The Occupation of Germany: New Light
        on How the Zones Were Drawn," Foreign Affairs,
XXVIII (July, 1950), 580-604.

741.   Nicholas, Herbert.   Britain and the U.S.A.   Balti-
        more: Johns Hopkins Press, 1963.

742.   Northedge, Frederick S.   British Foreign Policy:
        The Process of Readjustment, 1945-1961.   New York:
Praeger, 1962.

743.   Powers, Richard J., "Containment: From Greece to
        Vietnam--and Back? Western Political Quarterly,
XXII (December, 1969), 846-861.

744.   Roberts, Henry L. and Wilson, Paul A.   Britain and
        the United States: Problems in Cooperation.   A Joint

Report. New York: Published for the Council on Foreign
Relations by Herper, 1953.

745. Schick, John R.   The Berlin Crisis, 1958-1962.
      Philadelphia: University of Pennsylvania Press, 1971.

746. Smith, Jean Edward.   The Defense of Berlin.   Balti-
      more: Johns Hopkins Press, 1963.

747. Steel, Ronald.   The End of Alliance: America and
      the Future of Europe.   New York: Viking Press,
1964.

748. U. S. Congress. Senate.   Committee on Foreign
      Relations.   Documents on Germany, 1944-1959.
Washington: Government Printing Office, 1959.

749. U. S. Department of State.   The Axis in Defeat: A
      Collection of Documents on American Policy toward
Germany and Japan.   Washington: Government Printing
Office, 1945.

750. _____.   Occupation of Germany: Policy and
      Progress.   Washington: Government Printing Office,
1947.

751. _____.   Office of Public Affairs.   Germany, 1947-
      1949: The Story in Documents.   Washington: Govern-
ment Printing Office, 1950.

752. Warburg, James P.   Germany--Bridge or Battle-
      ground.   New York: Harcourt, Brace, 1947.

753. White, Theodore H.   Fire in the Ashes: Europe in
      Mid-Century.   New York: Sloane, 1953.

754. Woodhouse, Christopher M.   British Foreign Policy
      Since the Second World War.   New York: Praeger,
1962.

755. Xydis, Stephen G.   Greece and the Great Powers,
      1944-1947: Prelude to the "Truman Doctrine."
Thessaloniki: Institute for Balkan Studies, 1963.

756. Zink, Harold.   American Military Government in
      Germany.   New York: Macmillan, 1947.

757. _____. The United States in Germany, 1944-55.
      Princeton: Van Nostrand, 1957.

C. THE ENDING OF THE WAR

1. The Conferences: Yalta and Potsdam

758. Clemens, Diane Shaver. Yalta. New York: Oxford
      University Press, 1970.

759. Eden, Anthony. The Reckoning. Boston: Houghton
      Mifflin, 1965. Eden's Memoirs.

760. Feis, Herbert. Between War and Peace: The
      Potsdam Conference. Princeton: Princeton Univer-
sity Press, 1960.

761. _____. Churchill, Roosevelt, Stalin: The War
      They Waged and the Peace They Sought. Princeton:
Princeton University Press, 1957.

762. Pan, Stephen C. Y. , "Legal Aspects of the Yalta
      Agreement," American Journal of International Law,
LXVI (January, 1952), 40-59.

763. Rozek, Edward J. Allied Wartime Diplomacy: A
      Pattern in Poland. New York: Wiley, 1958.

764. Snell, John L. ed. The Meaning of Yalta: Big Three
      Diplomacy and the New Balance of Power. Baton
Rouge: Louisiana State University Press, 1956.

765. Sontag, Raymond J. "Reflections on the Yalta
      Papers," Foreign Affairs, XXXIII (July, 1955),
615-623.

766. Stettinius, Edward R. Roosevelt and the Russians:
      The Yalta Conference. Ed. by Walter Johnson.
Garden City: Doubleday, 1949.

767. Theoharis, Athan, "James F. Byrnes: Unwitting
      Yalta Myth-Maker," Political Science Quarterly,
LXXXI (December, 1966), 581-592.

768. _____. The Yalta Myths: An Issue in U. S.
      Politics, 1945-1955. Columbia: University of

Missouri Press, 1970.

769.   U. S. Department of State.   The Conference of Berlin
        (The Potsdam Conference), 1945.   Washington:
Government Printing Office, 1960.   2 vols.   (Foreign Relations of the United States, Diplomatic Papers).

770.   _____.   The Conferences at Malta and Yalta, 1945.
        Washington: Government Printing Office, 1955.
(Foreign Relations of the United States, Diplomatic Papers).

771.   Winnacker, Rudolph A. , "Yalta--Another Munich?"
        Virginia Quarterly Review, XXIV (Autumn, 1948),
521-537.

772.   Wittmer, Felix.   The Yalta Betrayal: Data on the
        Decline and Fall of Franklin Delano Roosevelt.
Caldwell, Ida: The Caxton Printers, 1953.

2.   The Atomic Bomb and Its Use

773.   Alperovitz, Gar.   Atomic Diplomacy: Hiroshima and
        Potsdam: The Use of the Atomic Bomb and the
American Confrontation with Soviet Power.   New York:
Simon & Schuster, 1965.

774.   _____.   Cold War Essays.   Garden City: Anchor
        Books, 1970.

775.   Amrine, Michael.   The Great Decision: The Secret
        History of the Atomic Bomb.   New York: Putnam's,
1959.

776.   Batchelder, Robert C.   The Irreversible Decision,
        1939-1950.   Boston: Houghton Mifflin, 1962.

777.   Blackett, Patrick M. S.   Fear, War and the Bomb:
        Military and Political Consequences of Atomic Energy.
New York: Whittlesey House, 1949.

778.   Bradley, David.   No Place to Hide.   Boston: Little,
        Brown, 1948.

779.   Brodie, Bernard, ed.   The Absolute Weapon: Atomic
        Power and World Order.   New York: Harcourt
Brace, 1946.

780.   Butow, Robert J. C. Japan's Decision to Surrender.
        Stanford: Stanford University Press, 1954.

781.   Coffey, Thomas M. Imperial Tragedy: Japan in
        World War II: The First Days and the Last. New
York: World, 1970.

782.   Compton, Arthur H. Atomic Quest: A Personal
        Narrative. New York: Oxford University Press,
1956.

783.   Compton, Karl T. , "If the Atomic Bomb Had Not
        Been Used," Atlantic Monthly, CLXXVIII (December,
1946), 54-56.

784.   Current, Richard N. Secretary Stimson: A Study in
        Statecraft. New Brunswick: Rutgers University
Press, 1954.

785.   Feis, Herbert. The Atomic Bomb and the End of
        World War II. Rev. ed. Princeton: Princeton
University Press, 1966.

786.   Giovannitti, Len and Freed, Fred. The Decision to
        Drop the Bomb. New York: Coward-McCann, 1965.

787.   Grew, Joseph C. Turbulent Era: A Diplomatic Record
        of Forty Years, 1904-1945. Boston: Houghton Mifflin,
1952. 2 vols. Vol. II.

788.   Hersey, John. Hiroshima. New York: Knopf, 1946.

789.   Kawai, Kazuo, "Mokusatsu, Japan's Response to the
        Potsdam Declaration," Pacific Historical Review,
XIX (November, 1950), 409-414.

790.   King, Ernest and Whitehill, Walter M. Fleet Ad-
        miral King: A Naval Record. New York: Norton,
1952.

791.   Knebel, Fletcher, and Bailey, Charles W. "The
        Fight over the A-Bomb," Look, XXVII (August 13,
1963), 19-23.

792.   _____. _____. No High Ground. New York:
        Harper, 1960.

793. Lamont, Lansing. Day of Trinity. New York:
      Atheneum, 1965.

794. Laurence, William L. Dawn over Zero: The Story
      of the Atomic Bomb. New York: Knopf, 1946.

795. Morison, Elting E. Turmoil and Tradition: The Life
      and Times of Henry L. Stimson. Boston: Houghton
Mifflin, 1960.

796. Morton, Louis, "The Decision to Use the Atomic
      Bomb," in Command Decisions. U. S. Department
of the Army. Office of Military History. Washington:
Government Printing Office, 1960.

797. Schoenberger, Walter S. Decision of Destiny.
      Athens: Ohio University Press, 1969.

798. Smith, Gaddis. American Diplomacy during the
      Second World War, 1941-1945. New York: Wiley,
1965.

799. Snowman, Daniel, "President Truman's Decision to
      Drop the First Atomic Bomb," Political Studies,
XIV (October, 1966), 365-373.

800. Stimson, Henry L. , "The Decision to Use the Atomic
      Bomb," Harpers Magazine, CXCIV (February, 1947),
97-107.

801. _____. , and Bundy, McGeorge. On Active Service
      in Peace and War. New York: Harper, 1948.

802. Truman, Harry S. Mr. Citizen. New York:
      Bernard Geis Associates, distributed by Random
House, 1960.

803. U. S. Strategic Bombing Survey. Japan's Struggle to
      End the War. [Washington: Government Printing
Office, 1946.] [Its Reports, Pacific War. 2]

804. "Was A-Bomb on Japan a Mistake? Unpublished
      Story of Fateful Argument 15 Years Ago." U. S.
News and World Report, XLIX (August 15, 1960), 62-78.

3. The War Crime Trials

805. Appleman, John A. Military Tribunals and Inter-
      national Crimes. Indianapolis: Bobbs-Merrill, 1954.

806. Bernstein, Victor H. Final Judgment: The Story of
      Nuremberg. New York: Boni & Gaer, 1947.

807. Biddle, Francis B. In Brief Authority. Garden
      City: Doubleday, 1962.

808. Bosch, William J. Judgment on Nuremberg: Ameri-
      can Attitudes toward the Major German War-Crime
Trials. Chapel Hill: University of North Carolina Press,
1970.

809. Brown, Delmer M. , "Instruction and Research:
      Recent Japanese Political and Historical Materials,"
American Political Science Review, XLIII (October, 1949),
1010-1017.

810. Calvocoressi, Peter. Nuremberg: The Facts, the
      Law and the Consequences. New York: Macmillan,
1948.

811. Davidson, Eugene. The Trial of the Germans: An
      Account of the Twenty-Two Defendants before the
International Military Tribunal at Nuremberg. New York:
Macmillan, 1966.

812. Falk, Richard A. , Kolko, Gabriel and Lifton, Robert
      Jay, eds. Crimes of War. New York: Random
House, 1971.

813. Gerhart, Eugene C. America's Advocate: Robert H.
      Jackson. Indianapolis: Bobbs-Merrill, 1958.

814. Glueck, Sheldon. The Nuremberg Trial and Aggres-
      sive War. New York: Knopf, 1946.

815. Heydecker, Joe J. and Leeb, Johannes. The Nurem-
      berg Trial: A History of Nazi Germany As Revealed
through the Testimony at Nuremberg. Cleveland: World,
1962. Tr. and ed. by R. A. Downie.

816. Horwitz, Solis, "The Tokyo Trial," International
      Conciliation, 465 (November, 1950), 473-584.

817.   Jackson, Robert H.   The Case against the Nazi War
       Criminals: Opening Statement for the United States
of America ... and Other Documents.   New York: Knopf,
1946.

818.   _____.   The Nürnberg Case: Together with Other
       Documents.   New York: Knopf, 1947.

819.   Keenan, Joseph B. and Brown, Brendan Francis.
       Crimes against International Law.   Washington:
Public Affairs Press, 1950.

820.   Knieriem, August von.   The Nuremberg Trials.
       Chicago: Regnery, 1959.   Tr. from the German.

821.   Peterson, Ted and Jensen, Jay W., "The Case of
       General Yamashita: A Study of Suppression,"
Journalism Quarterly, XXVIII (Spring, 1951), 196-212.

822.   Pompe, C. A.   Aggressive War an International
       Crime.   The Hague: Martinus Nijhoff, 1953.

823.   Reel, Adolf Frank.   The Case of General Yamashita.
       Chicago: University of Chicago Press, 1949.

824.   Sung, Yoon Cho, "The Tokyo War Crimes Trial,"
       Quarterly Journal of the Library of Congress, XXIV
(October, 1967), 309-318.

825.   Woetzel, Robert K.   The Nuremberg Trials in Inter-
       national Law, with a Postlude on the Eichmann Case.
New York: Praeger, 1962.

4.   The UN, Disarmament, and Peace

826.   Bechhoefer, Bernhard G.   Postwar Negotiations for
       Arms Control.   Washington: Brookings Institution,
1961.

827.   Beichman, Arnold.   The "Other" State Department:
       The United States Mission to the United Nations--Its
Role in the Making of Foreign Policy.   New York: Basic
Books, 1968.

828.   Besterman, Theodore.   UNESCO: Peace in the Minds
       of Men.   New York: Praeger, 1951.

829. Bloomfield, Lincoln P. and others. International
      Military Forces: The Question of Peacekeeping in an
Armed and Disarming World. Boston: Little, Brown, 1964.

830. _____. The United Nations and U. S. Foreign
      Policy: A New Look at the National Interest. Rev.
ed. Boston: Little, Brown, 1967.

831. Brennan, Donald J. , ed. Arms Control, Disarma-
      ment, and National Security. New York: Braziller,
1961.

832. Cohen, Bernard Cecil. The Political Process and
      Foreign Policy: The Making of the Japanese Peace
Settlement. Princeton: Princeton University Press, 1957.

833. Dean, Vera Micheles. The Four Cornerstones of
      Peace. New York: McGraw-Hill, 1946.

834. Dolivet, Louis. The United Nations: A Handbook on
      the New World Organization. New York: Farrar,
Straus, 1946.

835. Dunn, Frederick S. and others. Peace-Making and
      the Settlement with Japan, by Frederick S. Dunn,
Annemarie Shimony, Percy E. Corbett and Bernard C.
Cohen. Princeton: Princeton University Press, 1963.

836. _____. War and the Minds of Men. New York:
      Published for the Council on Foreign Relations by
Harper, 1950.

837. Goodrich, Leland M. , Hambro, Edward and Simons,
      Anne P. Charter of the United Nations: Commentary
and Documents. 3d and rev. ed. New York: Columbia
University Press, 1969.

838. _____. and Simons, Anne P. The United Nations
      and the Maintenance of International Peace and
Security. Washington: Brookings Institution, 1955.

839. Harley, John Eugene. Documentary Textbook on the
      United Nations: Humanity's March toward Peace ...
2d ed. rev. and enl. Los Angeles: Center for International Understanding, 1950.

840. Lane, Arthur Bliss. I Saw Poland Betrayed: An

American Ambassador Reports to the American
People. Indianapolis, Bobbs-Merrill, 1948.

841. Leiss, Amelia C. ed. European Peace Treaties
     after World War II: Negotiations and Texts of Treaties
with Italy, Bulgaria, Hungary, Rumania and Finland. Boston: World Peace Foundation, 1954. (Supplementary to
Documents on American Foreign Relations VIII, 1945-1946
and IX, 1947).

842. Lie, Trygve. In the Cause of Peace: Seven Years
     with the United Nations. New York: Macmillan,
1954.

843. Melman, Seymour, ed. Disarmament: Its Politics
     and Economics. Boston: American Academy of Arts
and Sciences, 1962.

844. Mikolajczyk, Stanislaw. The Rape of Poland: Pattern
     of Soviet Aggression. New York: McGraw-Hill,
1948.

845. Millis, Walter. An End to Arms. New York:
     Atheneum, 1965.

846. Nicholas, Herbert. The United Nations As a Political
     Institution. 3d ed. London: Oxford University
Press, 1967.

847. Opie, Redvers and others. The Search for Peace
     Settlements, by Redvers Opie, J. W. Ballantine,
Paul Birdsell, J. E. Muther and C. E. Thurber. Washington: Brookings Institution, 1951.

848. Paris Conference to Consider the Draft Treaties of
     Peace with Italy, Rumania, Bulgaria, Hungary and
Finland, 1946. Selected Documents. Washington: Government Printing Office, 1947.

849. Russell, Ruth B. and Muther, Jeannette E. A His-
     tory of the United Nations Charter: The Role of the
United States, 1940-1945. Washington: Brookings Institution, 1958.

850. _____. The United Nations and United States
     Security Policy. Washington: Brookings Institution,
1968.

851.   Schelling, Thomas C. and Halperin, Morton H.
        Strategy and Arms Control. New York: Twentieth
Century Fund, 1961.

852.   Slessor, Sir John. What Price Coexistence? A
        Policy for the Western Alliance. New York: Praeger,
1961.

853.   Toussaint, Charmian E. The Trusteeship System of
        the United Nations. New York: Praeger, 1956.
Published under the Auspices of the London Institute of
World Affairs.

854.   United Nations. Secretariat. The United Nations
        and Disarmament, 1945-1965. New York: United
Nations, 1967.

855.   U. S. Department of State. Making the Peace
        Treaties, 1941-1947. Washington: Department of
State, 1947.

856.   _____. Historical Office. Documents on Disarma-
        ment, 1945-1960. Washington: Government Printing
Office, 1960-61. 3 vols.

857.   Warburg, James P. Disarmament: The Challenge
        of the 1960's. Garden City: Doubleday, 1961.

858.   Wilcox, Francis O. and Haviland, H. Field, eds.
        The United States and the United Nations. Balti-
more: Johns Hopkins Press, 1961.

859.   Wittner, Lawrence. Rebels against War: The
        American Peace Movement, 1941-1960. New York:
Columbia University Press, 1969.

D.   THE COLD WAR

860.   Alperovitz, Gar. Atomic Diplomacy: Hiroshima and
        Potsdam: The Uses of the Atomic Bomb and the
American Confrontation with Soviet Power. New York:
Simon & Schuster, 1965.

861.   _____. Cold War Essays. Garden City: Anchor
        Books, 1970.

862. _____., "The Double Dealer," Review of The
      Secret Surrender by Allen W. Dulles, New York
Review of Books, VII (September 8, 1966), 3-4.

863. Aptheker, Herbert. American Foreign Policy and
      the Cold War. New York: New Century Publishers,
1962.

864. Aronson, James. The Press and the Cold War.
      Indianapolis: Bobbs-Merrill, 1970.

865. Barnet, Richard J. and Raskin, Marcus G. After
      20 Years: Alternatives to the Cold War in Europe.
New York: Random House, 1965.

866. Bell, Coral. Negotiation from Strength: A Study in
      the Politics of Power. New York: Knopf, 1963.

867. Beloff, Max, "No Peace, No War," Foreign Affairs,
      XXVII (January, 1949), 215-231.

868. Bouscaren, Anthony Trawick. Soviet Foreign Policy:
      A Pattern of Persistence. New York: Fordham
University Press, 1962.

869. Burnham, James. Containment or Liberation: An
      Inquiry into the Aims of United States Foreign Policy.
New York: Day, 1953.

870. _____. The Struggle for the World. New York:
      Day, 1947.

871. Carr, Albert H. Z. Truman, Stalin and Peace.
      Garden City: Doubleday, 1950.

872. Clay, Gen. Lucius D. Decision in Germany. Gar-
      den City: Doubleday, 1950.

873. _____. Germany and the Fight for Freedom.
      Cambridge: Harvard University Press, 1950.

874. Davison, Walter Phillips. The Berlin Blockade: A
      Study in Cold War Politics. Princeton: Princeton
University Press, 1958.

875. Dean, Vera Micheles. The United States and Russia.
      3d printing rev. Cambridge: Harvard University
Press, 1948.

876.   Deane, John R.   The Strange Alliance: The Story of
        Our Efforts at Wartime Co-operation with Russia.
New York: Viking Press, 1947.

877.   Dennett, Raymond and Johnson, Joseph E. , eds.
        Negotiating with the Russians.   Boston: World Peace
Foundation, 1951.

878.   Divine, Robert A. , "The Cold War and the Election
        of 1948," Journal of American History, LIX (June,
1972), 90-110.

879.   Druks, Herbert.   Harry S. Truman and the Russians,
        1945-1953.   New York: Robert Speller, 1967.

880.   Dulles, John Foster, "Security in the Pacific,"
        Foreign Affairs, XXX (January, 1952), 175-187.

881.   _____. War or Peace.   2d ed.   New York:
        Macmillan, 1957.

882.   Eisenhower, Dwight David.   Crusade in Europe.
        Garden City: Doubleday, 1948.

883.   Eliot, George Fielding.   If Russia Strikes --
        Indianapolis: Bobbs-Merrill, 1949.

884.   Feis, Herbert.   From Trust to Terror: The Onset
        of the Cold War, 1945-1950.   New York: Norton,
1970.

885.   Fleming, Denna Frank, ed. , "The Changing Cold
        War," American Academy of Political and Social
Science.   Annals, 351 (January, 1964), 1-180.

886.   _____. The Cold War and Its Origins, 1917-1960.
        Garden City: Doubleday, 1961.   2 vols.

887.   Fontaine, André.   History of the Cold War: From
        the October Revolution to the Korean War, 1917-1950.
New York: Pantheon Books, 1968.   (History of the Cold
War, Vol. I) Tr. from the French by D. D. Paige.

888.   _____. History of the Cold War: From the
        Korean War to the Present.   New York: Pantheon
Books, 1969.   (History of the Cold War, Vol. II) Tr. from
the French by Renaud Bruce.

889. Forrestal, James. The Forrestal Diaries. Ed. by
     Walter Millis. New York: Viking Press, 1951.

890. Fulbright, J. William, "Reflections: In Thrall to
     Fear," New Yorker, XLVII (January 8, 1972), 41-62.

891. Gabriel, Ralph H. , "The Cold War and Changes in
     American Thought," Virginia Quarterly Review,
XXXV (Winter, 1959), 53-63.

892. Gardner, Lloyd C. Architects of Illusion: Men and
     Ideas in American Foreign Policy, 1941-1949.
Chicago: Quadrangle Books, 1970.

893. Gati, Charles, "What Containment Meant," Foreign
     Policy No. 7 (Summer, 1972), 22-40.

894. Gavin, James M. War and Peace in the Space Age.
     New York: Harper, 1958.

895. Gerson, Louis L. The Hyphenate in Recent Ameri-
     can Politics and Diplomacy. Lawrence: University
of Kansas Press, 1964.

896. Graebner, Norman A. Cold War Diplomacy: Ameri-
     can Foreign Policy, 1945-1960. Princeton: Van
Nostrand, 1962.

897. _____. "The Truman Administration and the Cold
     War," Current History, XXXV (October, 1958), 223-
228.

898. Halle, Louis Joseph. The Cold War As History.
     New York: Harper, 1967.

899. Hammond, Paul Y. The Cold War Years: American
     Foreign Policy Since 1945. New York: Harcourt
Brace, 1969.

900. Hardt, John Pearce. , Stolzenbach, C. Darwin, and
     Kohn, Martin J. The Cold War Economic Gap: The
Increasing Threat to American Supremacy. New York:
Praeger, 1961.

901. Herring, George C. "Lend-Lease to Russia and the
     Origins of the Cold War, 1944-1945," Journal of
American History, LVI (June, 1969), 93-114.

902.   Herz, Martin F. The Beginnings of the Cold War.
        Bloomington: Indiana University Press, 1966.

903.   Hoffman, Paul G. Peace Can Be Won.   Garden City:
        Doubleday, 1951.

904.   Horowitz, David, ed. Containment and Revolution.
        Boston: Beacon Press, 1968. (Studies in Imperialism
and the Cold War, Vol. I).

905.   _____. , ed. Corporations and the Cold War.
        New York: Monthly Review Press, 1969. (Studies
in Imperialism and the Cold War, Vol. II).

906.   _____. The Free World Colossus: A Critique
        of American Foreign Policy in the Cold War.   New
York: Hill and Wang, 1965.

907.   _____. From Yalta to Vietnam: American Foreign
        Policy in the Cold War.   Rev. ed.   Harmondsworth:
Penguin, 1967.   Previous ed. published as The Free World
Colossus.

908.   Hughes, Henry Stuart. An Essay for Our Times.
        New York: Knopf, 1950.

909.   _____, "The Second Year of the Cold War,"
        Commentary, XLVIII (August, 1969), 27-32.

910.   Ingram, Kenneth. History of the Cold War.   New
        York: Philosophical Library, 1955.

911.   Kennan, George F. , "Interview with George F.
        Kennan," Foreign Policy No. 7 (Summer, 1972), 5-21.

912.   _____. On the Dealing with the Communist World.
        New York: Published for the Council on Foreign
Relations by Harper & Row, 1964.

913.   _____. Russia and the West under Lenin and
        Stalin. Boston: Little, Brown, 1961.

914.   _____. Russia, the Atom and the West.   New
        York: Harper, 1958.

915.   _____. (X, pseud.) "The Sources of Soviet Con-
        duct," Foreign Affairs, XXV (July, 1947), 566-582.

916.   Kieffer, John Elmer.   Strategy for Survival.   New
       York: McKay, 1953.

917.   Kolko, Joyce and Kolko, Gabriel.   The Limits of
       Power: The World and United States Foreign Policy,
1945-1954.   New York: Harper &   Row, 1972.

918.   LaFeber, Walter.   America, Russia, and the Cold
       War, 1945-1966.   New York: Wiley, 1967.

919.   Lasch, Christopher, "The Cold War Revisited and
       Revisioned," New York Times Magazine, (January 14,
1968), 26-27, 44, 46, 48.

920.   Lerche, Charles O.   The Cold War ... and After.
       Englewood Cliffs, N. J. , Prentice-Hall, 1965.

921.   Lippmann, Walter.   The Cold War: A Study in U. S.
       Foreign Policy.   New York: Harper, 1947.

922.   Luard, David E. T. , ed.   The Cold War: A Re-
       Appraisal.   New York: Praeger, 1964.

923.   Lukacs, John A.   A History of the Cold War.   Gar-
       den City: Doubleday, 1961.

924.   Lynd, Staughton, "How the Cold War Began,"
       Commentary, XXX (November, 1960), 379-389.

925.   McInnis, Edgar Wardwell.   The Atlantic Triangle
       and the Cold War.   Toronto: Published for the
Canadian Institute of International Affairs by the University
of Toronto Press, 1959.

926.   McNeill, William Hardy.   America, Britain and
       Russia: Their Cooperation and Conflict, 1941-1946.
New York: Oxford University Press, 1953.   (Survey of
International Affairs, 1941-1946, Vol. III) Issued under
the auspices of the Royal Institute of International Affairs.

927.   Madariaga, Salvador de.   The Blowing Up of the
       Parthenon: Or, How to Lose the Cold War.   New
York: Praeger, 1960.

928.   Marzani, Carl.   We Can Be Friends.   New York:
       Topical Book Publishers, 1952.

929.   Melby, John F. , "The Origins of the Cold War in
       China," Pacific Affairs, XLI (Spring, 1968), 19-33.

930.   Melman, Seymour. Our Depleted Society. New
       York: Holt, Rinehart & Winston, 1965.

931.   _____. The Peace Race. New York: Ballantine
       Books, 1961.

932.   Morray, Joseph P. From Yalta to Disarmament:
       Cold War Debate. New York: Monthly Review Press,
1961.

933.   Mowrer, Edgar Ansel. An End to Make-Believe.
       New York: Duell, Sloan and Pearce, 1961.

934.   Neumann, William L. After Victory: Churchill,
       Roosevelt, Stalin and the Making of the Peace. New
York: Harper & Row, 1967.

935.   Niebuhr, Reinhold. The Irony of American History.
       New York: Scribners, 1952.

936.   Parenti, Michael. The Anti-Communist Impulse.
       New York: Random House, 1970.

937.   Paterson, Thomas G. , "The Abortive American Loan
       to Russia and the Origins of the Cold War, 1943-
1946," Journal of American History, LVI (June, 1969),
70-92.

938.   _____. , ed. Cold War Critics: Alternatives to
       American Policy in the Truman Years. Chicago:
Quadrangle Books, 1971.

939.   Perla, Leo. Can We End the Cold War? A Study
       in American Foreign Policy. New York: Macmillan,
1960.

940.   Rapoport, Anatol. The Big Two: Soviet-American
       Perceptions of Foreign Policy. New York: Pegasus,
1971.

941.   Reitzel, William, Kaplan, Morton A. , and Coblenz,
       Constance G. , eds. United States Foreign Policy,
1945-1955. Washington: Brookings Institution, 1956.

942.   Roberts, Chalmers M. , "How Containment Worked,"
       Foreign Policy No. 7 (Summer, 1972), 41-53.

943.   Roberts, Henry L.   Russia and America: Dangers
       and Prospects.   New York: Published for the
Council on Foreign Relations by Harper, 1956.

944.   Rostow, Walt W.   The United States in the World
       Arena: An Essay in Recent History.   New York:
Harper, 1960.

945.   Schick, John R. , The Berlin Crisis, 1958-1962.
       Philadelphia: University of Pennsylvania Press, 1971.

946.   Schlesinger, Arthur M. and Alperovitz, Gar,
       "Letters," New York Review of Books, VII (Octo-
ber 20, 1966), 37-38.   This is a discussion of a review
written by Gar Alperovitz of The Secret Surrender by
Allen W. Dulles.

947.   _____. , "Origins of the Cold War," Foreign
       Affairs, XLVI (October, 1967), 22-52.

948.   _____.   The Vital Center: The Politics of Free-
       dom.   Boston: Houghton Mifflin, 1949.

949.   Schlesinger, James R.   The Political Economy of
       National Security: A Study of the Economic Aspects
of the Contemporary Power Struggle.   New York: Praeger,
1960.

950.   Schuman, Frederick L.   The Cold War: Retrospect
       and Prospect.   2d ed.   Baton Rouge: Louisiana
State University Press, 1967.   First published 1962.

951.   Seton-Watson, Hugh.   The East European Revolution.
       3d ed.   New York: Praeger, 1956.   First published
1951.

952.   _____.   From Lenin to Krushchev: The History of
       World Communism.   New York: Praeger, 1960.
Original edition published in 1953 under the title: From
Lenin to Malenkov.

953.   _____.   Neither War Nor Peace: The Struggle for
       Power in the Postwar World.   2d ed.   New York:
Praeger, 1962.

954.   Shub, Boris. The Choice. New York: Duell, Sloan
        and Pearce, 1950.

955.   Shulman, Marshall D. Stalin's Foreign Policy Re-
        appraised. Cambridge: Harvard University Press,
1963.

956.   Snell, John L. , "The Cold War: Four Contemporary
        Appraisals," American Historical Review, LXVIII
(October, 1962), 69-75.

957.   _____. Wartime Origins of the East-West
        Dilemma over Germany. New Orleans: The Hauser
Press, 1959.

958.   Sternberg, Fritz. How to Stop the Russians without
        War. New York: Day, 1948.

959.   Stone, Isidor F. The Truman Era: How the Cold
        War Started. Washington: Monthly Review Press,
1953.

960.   Strausz-Hupé, Robert, Kintner, William R. , and
        Possony, Stefan T. A Forward Strategy for
America. New York: Harper, 1961.

961.   Trefousse, Hans L. The Cold War: A Book of Docu-
        ments. New York: Putnam's, 1965.

962.   Ulam, Adam B. The Rivals: America and Russia
        Since World War II. New York: Viking Press, 1971.

963.   U. S. Congress. House. Committee on Foreign
        Affairs. Subcommittee on Europe. The Cold War:
Origins and Developments. Hearings, June 7, 11, 14 and
18, 1971. Washington: Government Printing Office, 1971.

964.   Warburg, James P. The United States in a Changing
        World: An Historical Analysis of American Foreign
Policy. New York: Putnam's, 1954.

965.   Warth, Robert D. Soviet Russia in World Politics.
        New York: Twayne Publishers, 1963.

966.   Weems, Miner L. , "The Containment Policy after
        Twenty Years, An Assessment. " Southern Quarterly,
V (January, 1967), 177-196.

967. Wilson, Thomas W. Cold War and Common Sense:
A Close Look at the Record of Communist Gains and
Failures and of Freedom's Fortunes in the Mid-Twentieth
Century. Greenwich, Conn.: New York Graphic Society,
1962.

968. Wolfers, Arnold, ed. Alliance Policy in the Cold
War. Baltimore: Johns Hopkins Press, 1959.

969. Wright, Theodore P., "The Origins of the Free
Elections Dispute in the Cold War," Western Political
Quarterly, XIV (December, 1961), 850-864.

970. Zacharias, Ellis M. and Farago, Ladislas. Behind
Closed Doors: The Secret History of the Cold War.
New York: Putnam's, 1950.

971. Ziff, William Bernard. Two Worlds: A Realistic
Approach to the Problem of Keeping the Peace.
New York: Harper, 1946.

E. THE KOREAN WAR

972. Allen, Richard C. Korea's Syngman Rhee: An
Unauthorized Portrait. Rutland, Vt., Charles E.
Tuttle, 1960.

973. Beloff, Max. Soviet Policy in the Far East, 1944-
1951. New York: Oxford University Press, 1953.

974. Berger, Carl. The Korea Knot: A Military-Political
History. 2d ed. Philadelphia: University of Pennsylvania Press, 1964. First published 1957.

975. Biderman, Albert D. March to Calumny: The Story
of American POW's in the Korean War. New York:
Macmillan, 1963.

976. Briggs, Ellis. Farewell to Foggy Bottom: The
Recollections of a Career Diplomat. New York:
McKay, 1964.

977. Cagle, Malcolm W. and Manson, Frank A. The Sea
War in Korea. Annapolis: United States Naval Institute, 1957.

978.   Caridi, Ronald J. , "The G. O. P. and the Korean
        War," Pacific Historical Review, XXXVII (November,
1968), 423-443.

979.   _____. The Korean War and American Politics:
        The Republican Party As a Case Study. Philadelphia:
University of Pennsylvania Press, 1969.

980.   Cho, Soon Sung. Korea in World Politics, 1940-1950;
        An Evaluation of American Responsibility. Berkeley:
University of California Press, 1967. (A Publication of the
Center for Japanese and Korean Studies).

981.   Clark, Mark Wayne. From the Danube to the Yalu.
        New York: Harper, 1954.

982.   Collins, Joseph Lawton. War in Peacetime: The
        History and Lessons of Korea. Boston: Houghton
Mifflin, 1969.

983.   Crofts, Alfred, "The Start of the Korean War Re-
        considered," Rocky Mountain Social Science Journal,
VII (April, 1970), 109-129.

984.   Fehrenbach, T. R. The Fight for Korea: From the
        War of 1950 to the Pueblo Incident. New York:
Grosset & Dunlap, 1969.

985.   _____. This Kind of War: A Study in Unpre-
        paredness. New York: Macmillan, 1967.

986.   Futrell, Robert Frank. The United States Air Force
        in Korea, 1950-1953. New York: Duell, Sloan and
Pearce, 1961.

987.   Geer, Andrew C. The New Breed: The Story of
        the U. S. Marines in Korea. New York: Harper,
1952.

988.   Goodrich, Leland M. Korea: A Study of U. S. Policy
        in the United Nations. New York: Council on Foreign
Relations, 1956.

989.   Gordenker, Leon, "The United Nations, the United
        States Occupation and the 1948 Election in Korea,"
Political Science Quarterly, LXXIII (September, 1958),
426-50.

990. Green, Adwin Wigfall. The Epic of Korea. Washing-
      ton: Public Affairs Press, 1950.

991. Gunther, John. The Riddle of MacArthur: Japan,
      Korea and the Far East. New York: Harper, 1951.

992. Halperin, Morton H. , "The Limiting Process in the
      Korean War," Political Science Quarterly, LXXVIII
(March, 1963), 13-39.

993. Hersey, John, "Profiles: Mr. President, II: Ten
      O'Clock Meeting," New Yorker, XXVII (April 14,
1951), 38-55.

994. _____, "Profiles: Mr. President, V: A Weighing
      of Words," New Yorker, XXVII (May 5, 1951), 36-53.

995. _____, "The Wayard Press: Conference in Room
      474," New Yorker, XXVI (December 16, 1950), 78-90.

996. Higgins, Trumbull. Korea and the Fall of MacArthur:
      A Précis in Limited War, New York: Oxford Univer-
sity Press, 1960.

997. Hoyt, Edwin C. , "United States Reaction to the
      Korean Attack: A Story of the Principles of the
United Nations Charter As a Factor in American Policy
Making," American Journal of International Law, LV
(January, 1961), 45-47.

998. Hunt, Frazier. The Untold Story of Douglas
      MacArthur. New York: Devin-Adair, 1954.

999. Joy, C. Turner. How Communists Negotiate. New
      York: Macmillan, 1955.

1000. Karig, Walter, Cagle, Malcolm W. and Manson,
      Frank A. Battle Report: The War in Korea. New
York: Rinehart, 1952. (Battle Report Vol. VI)

1001. Kie-Chiang Oh, John, "Role of the United States in
      South Korea's Democratization," Pacific Affairs,
XLIII (Summer, 1969), 164-177.

1002. Kinkead, Eugene. In Every War But One. New York:
      Norton, 1959.

1003.   Leckie, Robert.   Conflict: The History of the Korean
        War, 1950-1953.   New York: Putnam's, 1962.

1004.   Lee, Clark Gould and Henschel, Richard.   Douglas
        MacArthur.   New York: Holt, 1952.

1005.   Lofgren, Charles A. , "Mr. Truman's War: A Debate
        and Its Aftermath," Review of Politics, XXXI (April,
1969),   223-241.

1006.   Lyons, Gene M.   Military Policy and Economic Aid:
        The Korean Case, 1950-1953.   Columbus: Ohio State
University Press, 1961.

1007.   MacArthur, Douglas.   Reminiscences.   New York:
        McGraw-Hill, 1964.

1008.   _____.   Representative Speeches of General of the
        Army Douglas MacArthur, comp. by the Legislative
Reference Service, Library of Congress.   Washington:
Government Printing Office, 1964.   (88th Cong. , 2d Sess.
Senate. Doc. No. 95) [Serial No. 12622].

1009.   _____.   A Soldier Speaks: Public Papers and
        Speeches of General of the Army Douglas MacArthur.
New York: Praeger, 1965.

1010.   McCune, George M. and Grey, Arthur L.   Korea
        Today.   Cambridge: Harvard University Press, 1950.
Issued under the auspices of the International Secretariat,
Institute of Pacific Relations.

1011.   McLellan, David S. , "Dean Acheson and the Korean
        War," Political Science Quarterly, LXXXIII (March,
1968),   16-39.

1012.   Marshall, S. L. A.   Pork Chop Hill: The American
        Fighting Man in Action, Korea, Spring, 1953.   New
York: Morrow, 1956.

1013.   _____.   The River and the Gauntlet.   New York:
        Morrow, 1953.

1014.   Meade, Edward Grant.   American Military Govern-
        ment in Korea.   New York: King's Crown Press,
Columbia University, 1951.

1015.   Norman, John, "MacArthur's Blockade Proposals
        against Red China," Pacific Historical Review, XXVI
(May, 1957), 161-174.

1016.   Oliver, Robert T. Why War Came in Korea. New
        York: Fordham University Press, 1950.

1017.   Padelford, Norman J. , "The United Nations and
        Korea: A Political Resumé," International Organiza-
tion, V (November, 1951), 685-708.

1018.   Paige, Glenn D. The Korea Decision, June 24-30,
        1950. New York: Free Press, 1968.

1019.   Poats, Rutherford M. Decision in Korea. New
        York: McBride, 1954.

1020.   Rees, David. Korea: The Limited War. New York:
        St. Martin's Press, 1964.

1021.   Reeve, Wilfred Douglas. The Republic of Korea: A
        Political and Economic Study. New York: Oxford
University Press, 1963.

1022.   Ridgway, Matthew B. The Korean War: How We Met
        the Challenge. Garden City: Doubleday, 1967.

1023.   _____. and Martin, Harold H. Soldier: The
        Memoirs of Matthew B. Ridgway. New York:
Harper, 1956.

1024.   Rovere, Richard H. and Schlesinger, Arthur M. The
        General and the President and the Future of American
Foreign Policy. New York: Farrar, Straus & Young, 1951.

1025.   _____. _____. The MacArthur Controversy
        and American Foreign Policy. New York: Farrar,
Straus and Giroux, 1965. First published 1951 as The
General and the President. Additional material is included.

1026.   Ruetten, Richard T. , "General Douglas MacArthur's
        'Reconnaisance in Force:' The Rationalization of a
Defeat in Korea," Pacific Historical Review, XXXVI
(February, 1967), 79-93.

1027.   Snyder, Richard and Paige, Glenn D. , "The United
        States Decision to Resist Aggression in Korea: The

Application of an Analytical Scheme," in Foreign Policy
Decision Making: An Approach to the Study of International
Politics, ed. by Richard Snyder, H. W. Bruck and Burton
Sapin. New York: Free Press of Glencoe, 1962.

1028. Spanier, John W. The Truman-MacArthur Controversy
       and the Korean War. Cambridge: Belknap Press of
Harvard University, 1959.

1029. _____. The Truman-MacArthur Controversy and
       the Korean War. 2d ed. New York: Norton, 1965.

1030. Steinberg, Blema S. , "The Korean War: A Case
       Study in Indian Neutralism," Orbis, VIII (Winter,
1965), 937-954.

1031. Stone, Isidor F. The Hidden History of the Korean
       War. 2d ed. New York: Monthly Review Press,
1969c1952.

1032. U. S. Congress. Senate. Committee on Armed Ser-
       vices and the Committee on Foreign Relations. Mili-
tary Situation in the Far East: Hearings to Conduct an Inquiry
into the Military Situation in the Far East and the Facts Sur-
rounding the Relief of General of the Army Douglas MacArthur.
Pts. 1-5. Washington: Government Printing Office, 1951.
5 vols. (82d Cong. 1st Sess.)

1033. U. S. Department of State. The Korean Problem
       at the Geneva Conference, April 26-June 15,
1954. Washington: Government Printing Office, 1954.

1034. _____. North Korea: A Case Study in the Tech-
       niques of Takeover. Washington: Government Print-
ing Office, 1961. (Far Eastern Series 103).

1035. _____. Office of Public Affairs. United States
       Policy in the Korean Crisis. Washington: Govern-
ment Printing Office, 1950. (Far Eastern Series 34).

1036. U. S. Department of the Army. Historical Division.
       The United States Army in the Korean War. Washing-
ton: Government Printing Office, 1961-1966. 2 vols. The
beginning of the official history.

1037. U. S. Marine Corps. U. S. Marine Operations in

Korea, 1950-1953. Washington: U. S. Marine Corps Historical Branch, G-3, 1954-1962. 4 vols.

1038. Vatcher, William Henry. The Story of the Korean Military Armistice Negotiations. New York: Praeger, 1958.

1039. Whiting, Allen S. China Crosses the Yalu: The Decision to Enter the Korean War. New York: Macmillan, 1960.

1040. Whitney, Courtney. MacArthur: His Rendezvous with History. New York: Knopf, 1956.

1041. Willoughby, Charles A. and Chamberlain, John. MacArthur, 1941-1951. New York: McGraw-Hill, 1954.

1042. Wubben, H. H., "American Prisoners of War in Korea: A Second Look at the Something New in History Theme," American Quarterly, XXII (Spring, 1970), 3-19.

1043. Yoo, Tae-ho. The Korean War and the United Nations: A Legal and Diplomatic Historical Study. Louvain: Librairie Desbarax, 1965. (Université Catholique de Louvain).

IV. MILITARY POLICY IN THE ATOMIC AGE

A. GENERAL

1044. Baldwin, Hanson W. The Great Arms Race: A
       Comparison of U. S. and Soviet Power Today. New
York: Praeger, 1958.

1045. Borklund, Carl W. Men of the Pentagon: From
       Forrestal to McNamara. New York: Praeger, 1966.

1046. Brennan, Donald G. , ed. Arms Control, Disarma-
       ment, and National Security. New York: Braziller,
1961.

1047. Bush, Vannevar. Modern Arms and Free Men: A
       Discussion of the Role of Science in Preserving
Democracy. New York: Simon & Schuster, 1949.

1048. Caraley, Demetrios. The Politics of Military Unifi-
       cation: A Study of Conflict and the Policy Process.
New York: Columbia University Press, 1966.

1049. Cochran, Bert. The War System. New York:
       Macmillan, 1965.

1050. Connor, Sydney and Friedrich, Carl J. , eds. ,
       "Military Government," American Academy of
Political and Social Science. Annals, CCLXVII (January,
1950). All aspects covered in 20 articles.

1051. Cook, Fred J. The Warfare State. New York:
       Macmillan, 1962.

1052. Cutler, Robert, "The Development of the National
       Security Council," Foreign Affairs, XXXIV (April,
1956), 441-58.

1053. Ekirch, Arthur A. The Civilian and the Military.
       New York: Oxford University Press, 1956.

1054. Elliott, William Yandell. Mobilization Planning and the National Security, 1950-1960. Problems and Issues. Washington: Government Printing Office, 1950. (81st Cong., 2d Sess. Sen. Doc. 204).

1055. Falk, Stanley L., "The National Security Council under Truman, Eisenhower, and Kennedy," Political Science Quarterly, LXXIX (September, 1964), 403-434.

1056. Finletter, Thomas K. Power and Policy: U.S. Foreign Policy and Military Power in the Hydrogen Age. New York: Harcourt Brace., 1954.

1057. Hammond, Paul Y. "The National Security Council As a Device for Interdepartmental Coordination," American Political Science Review, LIV (December, 1960), 899-910.

1058. _____. Organizing for Defense: The American Military Establishment in the Twentieth Century. Princeton: Princeton University Press, 1961.

1059. Huntington, Samuel P., ed. Changing Patterns of Military Politics. Glencoe, Ill., Free Press of Glencoe, 1962.

1060. _____. The Common Defense: Strategic Programs in National Politics. New York: Columbia University Press, 1961.

1061. _____. The Soldier and the State: The Theory and Politics of Civil-Military Relations. Cambridge: Harvard University Press, 1957.

1062. Huzar, Elias. The Purse and the Sword: Control of the Army by Congress through Military Appropriations, 1933-1950. Ithaca: Cornell University Press, 1950.

1063. Jackson, Henry M., "To Forge a Strategy for Survival," Public Administration Review, XIX (Summer, 1959), 157-163.

1064. Javits, Jacob K., Hitch, Charles J. and Burns, Arthur F. The Defense Sector and the American Economy. New York: New York University Press, 1968. (The Charles C. Moskowitz Lectures, 8).

1065.   Kaufmann, William W. , ed.   Military Policy and
        National Security.   Princeton: Princeton University
Press, 1956.

1066.   Kecskemeti, Paul.   Strategic Surrender: The Politics
        of Victory and Defeat.   Stanford: Stanford University
Press, 1958.

1067.   Kerwin, Jerome Gregory, ed.   Civil-Military Relation-
        ships in American Life.   Chicago: University of
Chicago Press, 1948.

1068.   Kintner, William R. , Coffey, Joseph I. and Albright,
        Raymond J.   Forging a New Sword: A Study of the
Department of Defense.

1069.   Kissinger, Henry A.   The Necessity for Choice:
        Prospects of American Foreign Policy.   New York:
Harper, 1961.

1070.   _____.   Nuclear Weapons and Foreign Policy.   New
        York: Published for the Council on Foreign Relations
by Harper, 1957.

1071.   Kolodziej, Edward A.   The Uncommon Defense and
        Congress, 1945-1963.   Columbus: Ohio State Uni-
versity Press, 1966.

1072.   Lee, R. Alton, "The Army 'Mutiny' of 1946," Journal
        of American History, LIII (December, 1966), 555-571.

1073.   McClintock, Robert.   The Meaning of Limited War.
        Boston: Houghton Mifflin, 1967.

1074.   May, Ernest R. , "The Development of Political-
        Military Consultation in the United States," Political
Science Quarterly, LXX (June, 1955), 161-180.

1075.   Millis, Walter, Mansfield, Harvey C. , and Stein,
        Harold.   Arms and the State: Civil-Military Elements
in National Policy.   New York: Twentieth Century Fund,
1958.

1076.   Osgood, Robert E.   Limited War: The Challenge
        to American Strategy.   Chicago: University of
Chicago Press, 1957.

1077.   Peeters, Paul.   Massive Retaliation: The Policy and
        Its Critics.   Chicago: Regnery, 1959.

1078.   Ransom, Harry Howe.   Can American Democracy
        Survive Cold War?   Garden City: Doubleday, 1963.

1079.   Reinhardt, George C.   American Strategy in the
        Atomic Age.   Norman: University of Oklahoma Press,
1955.

1080.   Rogow, Arnold A.   James Forrestal: A Study of
        Personality, Politics, and Policy.   New York:
Macmillan, 1963.

1081.   Schilling, Warner R., Hammond, Paul Y., and
        Snyder, Glenn H.   Strategy, Politics and Defense
Budgets.   New York: Columbia University Press, 1962.

1082.   Schwarz, Urs.   American Strategy: A New Perspec-
        tive: The Growth of Politico-Military Thinking in the
United States.   New York: Doubleday, 1966.

1083.   Singer, Joel David.   Deterrence, Arms Control, and
        Disarmament: Toward a Synthesis in National Security
Policy.   Columbus: Ohio State University Press, 1962.

1084.   Smith, Bruce L. R.   The RAND Corporation: Case
        Study of a Nonprofit Advisory Corporation.   Cam-
bridge: Harvard University Press, 1966.

1085.   Smith, Louis.   American Democracy and Military
        Power: A Study of Civil Control of the Military Power
in the United States.   Chicago: University of Chicago Press,
1951.

1086.   Snyder, Glenn H.   Deterrence and Defense: Toward
        a Theory of National Security.   Princeton: Princeton
University Press, 1961.

1087.   Stanley, Timothy W.   American Defense and National
        Security.   Washington: Public Affairs Press, 1956.

1088.   Stein, Harold, ed.   American Civil-Military Decisions:
        A Book of Case Studies.   University: Published in
cooperation with the Inter-University Case Program by University of Alabama Press, 1963.

1089.   Swomley, John M.   The Military Establishment.
        Boston: Beacon Press, 1964.

1090.   Taylor, Maxwell D.   The Uncertain Trumpet.   New
        York: Harper & Row, 1960.

1091.   Turner, Gordon B. and Challener, Richard D. , eds.
        National Security in the Nuclear Age: Basic Facts
and Theories.   New York: Praeger, 1960.

1092.   Wallace, Donald H.   Economic Controls and Defense.
        New York: Twentieth Century Fund, 1953.

1093.   Waskow, Arthur I.   The Limits of Defense.   Garden
        City: Doubleday, 1962.

1094.   Yarmolinsky, Adam.   The Military Establishment:
        Its Impacts on American Society.   New York:
Harper & Row, 1971.

1095.   York, Herbert.   Race to Oblivion: A Participant's
        View of the Arms Race.   New York: Simon &
Schuster, 1970.

B.   ATOMIC ENERGY

1096.   Coale, Ansley J.   The Problem of Reducing Vulner-
        ability to Atomic Bombs.   Princeton: Princeton
University Press, 1947.

1097.   Cousins, Norman, and Finletter, Thomas K. , "A
        Beginning for Sanity," Saturday Review of Literature,
XXIX (June 15, 1946), 5-9, 38-40.

1098.   _____.   Modern Man Is Obsolete.   New York:
        Viking Press, 1945.

1099.   Curtis, Charles P.   The Oppenheimer Case: The
        Trial of a Security System.   New York: Simon &
Schuster, 1955.

1100.   Dean, Gordon E.   Report on the Atom: What You
        Should Know about the Atomic Energy Program of
the United States.   New York: Knopf, 1953.

1101.   Fermi, Laura (Capon).   Atoms for the World: United

States Participation in the Conference on the Peaceful Uses of Atomic Energy. Chicago: University Press, 1957.

1102. Green, Harold P. , and Rosenthal, Alan. _Government of the Atom: The Integration of Powers._ New York: Atherton Press, 1963.

1103. Groves, Leslie R. _Now It Can Be Told: The Story of the Manhattan Project._ New York: Harper & Row, 1962.

1104. Hewlett, Richard G. and Anderson, Oscar E. _A History of the United States Atomic Energy Commission._ University Park: Pennsylvania State University Press, 1962-1969. 2 vols. Vol. I. The New World, 1939/1946. Vol. II. Atomic Shield, 1947/1952.

1105. Jungk, Robert. _Brighter Than a Thousand Suns._ Tr. by James Cleugh. New York: Harcourt, Brace, 1958.

1106. Kramish, Arnold. _The Peaceful Atom in Foreign Policy._ New York: Published for the Council on Foreign Relations by Harper & Row, 1963.

1107. Lang, Daniel. _The Man in the Thick Lead Suit._ New York: Oxford University Press, 1954.

1108. Lapp, Ralph E. _Atoms and People._ New York: Harper, 1956.

1109. _____. _The New Force: The Story of Atoms and People._ New York: Harper, 1953.

1110. _____. _The Voyage of the Lucky Dragon._ New York: Harper, 1958.

1111. Lewis, Richard S. , Wilson, Jane, and Rabinowitch, Eugene, eds. _Alamagordo Plus Twenty-five Years: The Impact of Atomic Energy on Science, Technology, and World Politics._ New York: Viking Press, 1971.

1112. Lilienthal, David E. _Change, Hope, and the Bomb._ Princeton: Princeton University Press, 1963.

1113. _____. _Journals of David E. Lilienthal._ New York: Harper & Row, 1964-1971. 5 vols.

1114.   Newman, James R. and Miller, Byron S.   The Con-
            trol of Atomic Energy: A Study of Its Social, Economic
and Political Implications.   New York: McGraw-Hill, 1948.

1115.   Nieburg, Harold L.   Nuclear Secrecy and Foreign
            Policy.   Washington: Public Affairs Press, 1964.

1116.   Nogee, Joseph L.   Soviet Policy toward International
            Control of Atomic Energy.   Notre Dame, Ind.,
University of Notre Dame Press, 1961.

1117.   Tate, Merz and Hull, Doris M., "Effects of Nuclear
            Explosions on Pacific Islanders," Pacific Historical
Review, XXXIII (November, 1964), 379-393.

1118.   Teller, Edward.   Our Nuclear Future: Facts, Dangers
            and Opportunities.   New York: Criterion Books, 1958.

1119.   U.S. Atomic Energy Commission.   In the Matter of
            J. Robert Oppenheimer, Transcript of Hearing ...
April 12, 1954 through May 6, 1954.   Washington: Government Printing Office, 1954.

1120.   U.S. Congress.   Joint Committee on Atomic Energy.
            Atomic Power and Private Enterprise.   Washington:
Government Printing Office, 1952.   (82d Cong., 2d Sess.).

1121.   _____. _____.   Peaceful Uses of Atomic
            Energy.   Report of the Panel on the Impact of the
Peaceful Uses of Atomic Energy.   Washington: Government
Printing Office, 1956.   2 vols.   (84th Cong., 2d Sess.).

1122.   U.S. Department of State.   The International Control
            of Atomic Energy: Growth of a Policy.   Washington:
Government Printing Office, 1946.

1123.   _____.   The International Control of Atomic
            Energy: Policy at the Crossroads.   Washington:
Government Printing Office, 1948.   (General Foreign Policy
Series 3).

C.   NUCLEAR WARFARE

1124.   Arneson, R. Gordon, "The H-Bomb Decision,"
            Foreign Service Journal, XLVI (May, 1969), 27-29,
(June, 1969), 24-27, 43.

1125. Beaufre, André. Deterrence and Strategy. Tr. from
the French by R. H. Barry. New York: Praeger,
1966.

1126. Bennett, John C. , Ed. Nuclear Weapons and the
Conflicts of Conscience. New York: Scribner's,
1962.

1127. Blackett, Patrick M. S. Atomic Weapons and East-
West Relations. Cambridge: Cambridge University
Press, 1956.

1128. _____. , "Nuclear Weapons and Defence: Comments
on Kissinger, Kennan and King-Hall," International
Affairs, XXXIV (October, 1958), 421-434.

1129. _____. Studies of War, Nuclear and Conventional.
New York: Hill and Wang, 1962.

1130. Brodie, Bernard. Strategy in the Missile Age.
Princeton: Princeton University Press, 1959.

1131. Bulletin of the Atomic Scientists. The Atomic Age:
Scientists in National and World Affairs. Articles
from the Bulletin of Atomic Scientists, 1945-1962. Ed. by
Morton M. Grodzins and Eugene Rabinowitch. New York:
Basic Books, 1963.

1132. Davis, Elmer. Two Minutes till Midnight. Indianapolis: Bobbs-Merrill, 1955.

1133. Gallois, Pierre M. , The Balance of Terror: Strategy
for the Nuclear Age. Boston: Houghton Mifflin,
1961. Tr. from the French by Raymond Aron.

1134. Gilpin, Robert. American Scientists and Nuclear
Weapons Policy. Princeton: Princeton University
Press, 1962.

1135. Halle, Louis Joseph. Choice for Survival. New
York: Harper, 1958.

1136. Halperin, Morton H. Limited War in the Nuclear
Age. New York: Wiley, 1963.

1137. Kahn, Herman. On Thermonuclear War. 2d ed.
New York: Free Press, 1969. First published in

1960, Princeton University Press.

1138. _____. Thinking about the Unthinkable. New
York: Horizon Press, 1962.

1139. Knorr, Klaus and Read, Thornton, eds. Limited
Strategic War. New York: Praeger, 1962. (Prince-
ton University. Center of International Studies. Princeton
Studies in World Politics.)

1140. _____. On the Uses of Military Power in the
Nuclear Age. Princeton: Published for the Prince-
ton Center of International Studies by Princeton University
Press, 1966.

1141. Laird, Melvin R. A House Divided: America's
Strategy Gap. Chicago: Regnery, 1962.

1142. Lieberman, Joseph I. The Scorpion and the Taran-
tula: The Struggle to Control Atomic Weapons, 1945-
1949. Boston: Houghton Mifflin, 1970.

1143. Madariaga, Salvador de. The Blowing Up of the
Parthenon: Or How to Lose the Cold War. New York:
Praeger, 1960.

1144. Morgenstern Oskar. The Question of National
Defense. New York: Random House, 1959.

1145. Murray, Thomas E. Nuclear Policy for War and
Peace. Cleveland: World, 1960.

1146. Oppenheimer, J. Robert. "Atomic Weapons and
American Policy," Foreign Affairs, XXXI (July,
1953), 525-535.

1147. Roberts, Chalmers M. The Nuclear Years: The
Arms Race and Arms Control, 1945-1970. New
York: Praeger, 1970.

1148. Schilling, Warner R., "The H-Bomb Decision: How
to Decide without Actually Choosing," Political
Science Quarterly, LXXVI (March, 1961), 24-46.

1149. Shepley, James R. and Blair, Clay. The Hydrogen
Bomb: The Men, the Menace, the Mechanism. New
York: McKay, 1954.

1150.   Slessor, Sir John Cotesworth.   Strategy for the West.
        New York: Morrow, 1954.

1151.   Strauss, Lewis L.   Men and Decisions.   Garden City:
        Doubleday, 1962.

1152.   Teller, Edward and Brown, Allen.   The Legacy of
        Hiroshima.   Garden City: Doubleday, 1962.

1153.   Tucker, Robert W.   The Just War: A Study in Con-
        temporary American Doctrine.   Baltimore: Johns
Hopkins Press, 1960.

1154.   Twining, Nathan F.   Neither Liberty Nor Safety: A
        Hard Look at U.S. Military Policy and Strategy.
New York: Holt, Rinehart and Winston, 1966.

1155.   U.S. Department of Defense.   The Effects of Nuclear
        Weapons.   Rev. ed.   Washington: U.S. Atomic Energy
Commission, 1962.   Issued in 1957 by the U.S. Atomic
Defense Agency.

D.   THE NORTH ATLANTIC TREATY ORGANIZATION

1156.   Beaufre, André.   NATO and Europe.   Tr. from the
        French by Joseph Green.   New York: Knopf, 1966.

1157.   Buchan, Alastair.   NATO in the 1960's: The Impli-
        cations of Interdependence.   Rev. ed.   New York:
Published for the Institute for Strategic Studies by Praeger,
1963.

1158.   Calleo, David P.   The Atlantic Fantasy: The U.S.,
        NATO, and Europe.   Baltimore: Johns Hopkins
Press, 1970.

1159.   Fox, William T. R. and Fox, Annette B.   NATO
        and the Range of American Choice.   New York:
Columbia University Press, 1967.

1160.   Hoskins, Halford L.   The Atlantic Pact.   Washington:
        Public Affairs Press, 1949.

1161.   Kaplan, Lawrence A., "The United States and the
        Origins of NATO," Review of Politics, XXXI (April,
1969), 210-222.

1162.   Knorr, Klaus Eugen, ed.   NATO and American
        Security.   Princeton: Princeton University Press,
1959.

1163.   Krout, John A. , ed.   "The United States and the
        Atlantic Community," Academy of Political Science
Proceedings, XXIII (May, 1949), 221-342.

1164.   Middleton, Drew.   The Defense of Western Europe.
        New York: Appleton-Century-Crofts, 1952.

1165.   Osgood, Robert E.   NATO, The Entangling Alliance.
        Chicago: University of Chicago Press, 1962.

1166.   Richardson, James L.   Germany and the Atlantic
        Alliance: The Interaction of Strategy and Politics.
Cambridge: Harvard University Press, 1966.

1167.   Stikker, Dirk U.   Men of Responsibility: A Memoir.
        New York: Harper & Row, 1965.

V. DOMESTIC AFFAIRS

A. LOYALTY AND SECURITY

1. General

1168. Abbott, Roger S. , "The Federal Loyalty Program:
Background and Problems," American Political
Science Review, XLII (June, 1948), 486-499.

1169. Anderson, Dillon, "The President and the National
Security," Atlantic Monthly, CXCVII (January, 1956),
42-46.

1170. Andrews, Bert. Washington Witch Hunt. New York:
Random House, 1948.

1171. Arnold, Thurman, "How Not to Get Investigated, Ten
Commandments for Government Employees," Harper's
CXCVII (November, 1948), 61-63.

1172. Association of the Bar of the City of New York.
Special Committee on the Federal Loyalty-Security
Program. Report. New York: Dodd, Mead, 1956.

1173. Barth, Alan. Government by Investigation. New
York: Viking Press, 1955.

1174. _____. The Loyalty of Free Men. New York:
Viking Press, 1951.

1175. Bentley, Eric, ed. Thirty Years of Treason: Ex-
cerpts from Hearings before the House Committee
on Un-American Activities, 1938-1968. New York: Viking
Press, 1971.

1176. Bontecou, Eleanor. The Federal Loyalty-Security
Program. Ithaca: Cornell University Press, 1953.

1177. Brown, Ralph S. Loyalty and Security: Employment

101

         Tests in the United States. New Haven: Yale University Press, 1958.

1178. Buckley, William F. and the Editors of the *National Review*. *The Committee and Its Critics: A Calm Review of the House Committee on Un-American Activities*. New York: Putnam's, 1962.

1179. Carr, Robert K. *The House Committee on Un-American Activities*. Ithaca: Cornell University Press, 1952.

1180. Chase, Harold W. *Security and Liberty: The Problem of Native Communists, 1947-1955*. Garden City: Doubleday, 1955.

1181. Commager, Henry Steele, "Who is Loyal to America?" *Harper's Magazine*, CXCV (September, 1947), 193-199.

1182. Donovan, William J. and Jones, Mary G, "Program for a Democratic Counter Attack to Communist Penetration of Government Service," *Yale Law Journal*, LVIII (July, 1949), 1211-1241.

1183. Emerson, Thomas I. and Helfeld, David M. , "Loyalty among Government Employees," *Yale Law Journal*, LVIII (December 1948), 1-143.

1184. _____. _____. Reply by the authors [to "A Comment by J. Edgar Hoover on the article 'Loyalty among Government Employees.'"] *Yale Law Journal*, LVIII (February, 1949), 412-421.

1185. Ernst, Morris L. "Some Affirmative Suggestions for a Loyalty Program," *American Scholar*, XIX (Autumn, 1950), 452-460.

1186. Fellman, David. *The Defendant's Rights*. New York: Rinehart, 1958.

1187. Flynn, John T. *The Lattimore Story*. New York: Devin-Adair, 1953.

1188. _____. *While You Slept: Our Tragedy in Asia and Who Made It*. New York: Devin-Adair, 1951.

1189. Freeland, Richard M. *The Truman Doctrine and*

the Origins of McCarthyism: Foreign Policy, Domestic
Politics, and Internal Security, 1946-1948. New York: Knopf,
1972.

1190.   Gellhorn, Walter, "Report on a Report of the House
        Committee on Un-American Activities," Harvard Law
Review, LX (October, 1947), 1193-1234.

1191.   _____. Security, Loyalty, and Science. Ithaca:
        Cornell University Press, 1950.

1192.   _____, ed. The States and Subversion. Ithaca:
        Cornell University Press, 1952.

1193.   Gillmor, Dan. Fear, the Accuser. New York:
        Abelard-Schuman, 1954.

1194.   Goodman, Walter. The Committee: The Extraordinary
        Career of the House Committee on Un-American
Activities. New York: Farrar, Straus and Giroux, 1968.

1195.   Grodzins, Morton M. The Loyal and the Disloyal:
        Social Boundaries of Patriotism and Treason.
Chicago: University of Chicago Press, 1956.

1196.   Harper, Alan D. The Politics of Loyalty: The
        White House and the Communist Issue, 1946-1952.
Westport, Conn.: Greenwood Publishing Corporation, 1969.

1197.   Hofstadter, Richard. The Paranoid Style in American
        Politics and Other Essays. New York: Knopf, 1965.

1198.   Hoover, J. Edgar, "A Comment on the Article
        'Loyalty among Government Employees,'" Yale
Law Journal, LVIII (February, 1949), 401.

1199.   Jackson, Gabriel, "Reflections on Two Loyalty
        Purges," Centennial Review of Arts and Science,
IV (Spring, 1960), 223-242.

1200.   Lamont, Corliss. Freedom Is As Freedom Does:
        Civil Liberties Today. New York: Horizon Press,
1956.

1201.   Lattimore, Owen. Ordeal by Slander. Boston:
        Little, Brown, 1950.

1202.   McWilliams, Carey. Witch Hunt: The Revival of
        Heresy. Boston: Little, Brown, 1950.

1203.   Miller, Merle. The Judges and the Judged. [Report
        for the American Civil Liberties Union]. Garden
City: Doubleday, 1952.

1204.   Monroney, A. S. Mike and others. The Strengthening
        of American Political Institutions. Ithaca: Cornell
University Press, 1949.

1205.   Nikoloric, Leonard A. , "The Government Loyalty
        Program," American Scholar, XIX (Summer, 1950),
285-298.

1206.   O'Brian, John Lord, "Loyalty Tests and Guilt by
        Association," Harvard Law Review, LXI (April, 1948),
592-611.

1207.   Oxnam, G. Bromley. I Protest. New York: Har-
        per, 1954.

1208.   Reeves, Thomas C. Freedom and the Foundation:
        The Fund for the Republic in the Era of McCarthyism.
New York: Knopf, 1969.

1209.   Schaar, John H. Loyalty in America. Berkeley:
        University of California Press, 1957.

1210.   Shattuck, Henry L. , "The Loyalty Review Board of
        the U. S. Civil Service Commission, 1947-1953,"
Massachusetts Historical Society Proceedings, LXXVIII (1966),
63-80.

1211.   Shils, Edward A. The Torment of Secrecy, The
        Background and Consequences of American Security
Policies. Glencoe, Ill. , Free Press, 1956.

1212.   Stouffer, Samuel A. Communism, Conformity, and
        Civil Liberties: A Cross-Section of the Nation Speaks
Its Mind. Garden City: Doubleday, 1955.

1213.   Sutherland, Arthur E. , "Freedom and Internal
        Security," Harvard Law Review, LXIV (January,
1951), 383-416.

1214.   Taylor, Telford. Grand Inquest: The Story of

Congressional Investigations. New York: Simon &
Schuster, 1955.

1215.   U. S. Commission on Government Security.   Report.
Washington: Government Printing Office, 1957.

1216.   U. S. Congress. Senate. Internal Security Manual.
Rev. ed. to Jan. 1, 1961. Washington: Government
Printing Office, 1961. (86th Cong. , 2d Sess. Sen. Doc. 126).

1217.   _____. _____. Committee on Foreign Relations.   State Department Employee Loyalty Investigation. Washington: Government Printing Office, 1950. (81st
Cong. , 2d Sess. Senate Report 2108).

1218.   Wechsler, James A. The Age of Suspicion. New
York: Random House, 1953.

1219.   Weyl, Nathaniel. The Battle against Disloyalty. New
York: Crowell, 1951.

1220.   Wittenberg, Philip. The Lamont Case: History of a
Congressional Investigation. New York: Horizon
Press, 1957.

2.   The Communist Threat

1221.   Almond, Gabriel A. , Krugman, Herbert E. , Lewin,
Elizabeth and Wriggins, Howard. The Appeals of
Communism. Princeton: Princeton University Press, 1954.

1222.   Bentley, Elizabeth. Out of Bondage: The Story of
Elizabeth Bentley. New York: Devin-Adair, 1951.

1223.   Budenz, Louis F. Men without Faces: The Communist Conspiracy in the U. S. A. New York: Harper,
1950.

1224.   Burnham, James. The Coming Defeat of Communism.
New York: Day, 1950.

1225.   _____. The Web of Subversion: Underground Net-
works in the U. S. Government. New York: Day,
1954.

1226.   Corker, Charles, comp. Digest of the Public Record
of Communism in the United States. New York:

Fund for the Republic, 1955.

1227.   Dodd, Thomas J.   Freedom and Foreign Policy.
        New York: Bookmailer, 1962.

1228.   Ernst, Morris L. and Loth, David G.   Report on
        the American Communist.   New York: Holt, 1952.

1229.   Fast, Howard Melvin.   The Naked God: The Writer
        and the Communist Party.   New York: Praeger,
1957.

1230.   Hicks, Granville.   Where We Came Out.   New York:
        Viking Press, 1954.

1231.   Hook, Sidney.   Heresy, Yes--Conspiracy, No.   New
        York: Day, 1953.

1232.   Hoover, J. Edgar.   Masters of Deceit: The Story of
        Communism in America and How to Fight It.   New
York: Holt, Rinehart and Winston, 1958.

1233.   Howe, Irving and Coser, Louis.   The American Com-
        munist Party: A Critical History (1919-1957).   Boston:
Beacon Press, 1957.

1234.   Kahn, Gordon.   Hollywood on Trial: The Story of the
        10 Who Were Indicted.   New York: Boni & Gaer,
1948.

1235.   Kampelman, Max M.   The Communist Party vs.
        the C. I. O. : A Study in Power Politics.   New York:
Praeger, 1957.

1236.   Latham, Earl.   The Communist Controversy in
        Washington: From the New Deal to McCarthy.
Cambridge: Harvard University Press, 1966.

1237.   MacIver, Robert.   Academic Freedom in Our Time.
        New York: Columbia University Press, 1955.

1238.   Matusow, Harvey Marshall.   False Witness.   New
        York: Cameron & Kahn, 1955.

1239.   Meyer, Frank S.   The Moulding of Communists:
        The Training of the Communist Cadre.   New York:
Harcourt, Brace, 1961.

1240.   Miller, Merle. The Judges and the Judged: [Report
        for the American Civil Liberties Union.] Garden
City: Doubleday, 1952.

1241.   Packer, Herbert L. Ex-Communist Witnesses: Four
        Studies in Fact Finding. Stanford: Stanford Univer-
sity Press, 1962.

1242.   Parenti, Michael. The Anti-Communist Impulse.
        New York: Random House, 1970.

1243.   Philbrick, Herbert Arthur. I Led 3 Lives. New
        York: McGraw-Hill, 1952.

1244.   Posnack, Emanuel R. World without Barriers: A
        Perspective View of Our Present and Future in a
World of Economic and Ideological Conflict. New York:
Morrow, 1956.

1245.   Roy, Ralph Lord. Communism and the Churches.
        New York: Harcourt, Brace, 1960.

1246.   Saposs, David J. Communism in American Politics.
        Washington: Public Affairs Press, 1960.

1247.   _____. Communism in American Unions. New
        York: McGraw-Hill, 1959.

1248.   Seton-Watson, Hugh. Nationalism and Communism:
        Essays, 1946-1963. New York: Praeger, 1964.

1249.   _____. The Pattern of Communist Revolution: A
        Historical Analysis. Rev. enl. ed. London:
Methuen, 1960. First published 1953.

1250.   Shannon, David A. The Decline of American Com-
        munism: A History of the Communist Party of the
United States Since 1945. New York: Harcourt, Brace and
World, 1959.

1251.   Somerville, John MacPherson. The Communist
        Trials and the American Tradition: Expert Testimony
on Force and Violence. New York: Cameron Associates,
1956.

1252.   Starobin, Joseph R. American Communism in Crisis,
        1943-1957. Cambridge: Harvard University Press,
1972.

1253.   Stouffer, Samuel A.   Communism, Conformity, and
        Civil Liberties: A Cross-Section of the Nation Speaks
Its Mind.   Garden City: Doubleday, 1955.

1254.   Stripling, Robert E.   The Red Plot against America.
        Drexel Hill, Pa.: Bell Publishing Company, 1949.

1255.   U. S. Congress.   Senate.   Committee on Government
        Operations.   Congressional Investigations of Com-
munism and Subversive Activities: Summary-Index 1918 to
1956.   Washington: Government Printing Office, 1956.
(84th Cong., 2d Sess., Sen. Doc. No. 148) [Serial No.
11914.]

1256.   Welch, Robert.   The Politician.   Belmont, Mass.:
        Belmont Publishing Company, 1964.

3.   The Alger Hiss Case

1257.   Chambers, Whittaker.   Odyssey of a Friend: Whittaker
        Chambers' Letters to William F. Buckley, Jr. 1954-
1961.   New York: Putnam's, 1970.

1258.   _____.   Witness.   New York: Random House,
        1952.

1259.   Cook, Fred J.   The Unfinished Story of Alger Hiss.
        New York: Morrow, 1958.

1260.   Cooke, Alistair.   A Generation on Trial: U. S. A. v.
        Alger Hiss.   2d ed. enl.   New York: Knopf, 1952.

1261.   De Toledano, Ralph and Lasky, Victor.   Seeds of
        Treason: The True Story of the Hiss-Chambers
Tragedy.   New York: Published for Newsweek by Funk &
Wagnalls, 1950.

1262.   Hiss, Alger.   In the Court of Public Opinion.   New
        York: Knopf, 1957.

1263.   Jowitt, William Allen Jowitt, 1st earl.   The Strange
        Case of Alger Hiss.   Garden City: Doubleday, 1953.

1264.   Zeligs, Meyer A.   Friendship and Fratricide: An
        Analysis of Whittaker Chambers and Alger Hiss.
New York: Viking Press, 1967.

4. The Rise and Fall of Senator McCarthy

1265. Anderson, Jack and May, Ronald W. McCarthy: The
       Man, the Senator, the "Ism." Boston: Beacon
Press, 1952.

1266. Buckley, William F. and Bozell, L. Brent. McCarthy
       and His Enemies: The Record and Its Meaning.
Chicago: Regnery, 1954.

1267. Cohn, Roy. McCarthy. New York: New American
       Library, 1968.

1268. Cook, Fred J. The Nightmare Decade: The Life and
       Times of Senator Joe McCarthy. New York: Random
House, 1971.

1269. De Antonio, Emile and Talbot, Daniel. Point of
       Order! A Documentary of the Army-McCarthy
Hearings. New York: Norton, 1964.

1270. De Santis, Vincent P., "American Catholics and
       McCarthyism," Catholic Historical Review, LI
(April, 1965), 1-30.

1271. Fiedler, Leslie A. An End to Innocence: Essays on
       Culture and Politics. Boston: Beacon Press, 1955.

1272. Griffith, Robert, "The Political Context of
       McCarthyism," Review of Politics, XXXIII (January,
1971), 24-35.

1273. _____. The Politics of Fear: Joseph R. McCarthy
       and the Senate. Lexington: University Press of
Kentucky, 1970.

1274. Lokos, Lionel. Who Promoted Peress? New York:
       Bookmailer, 1961.

1275. McCarthy, Joseph R. America's Retreat from
       Victory: The Story of George Catlett Marshall. New
York: Devin-Adair, 1954.

1276. _____. McCarthyism: The Fight for America:
       Documented Answers to Questions Asked by Friend
and Foe. New York: Devin-Adair, 1952.

1277.   Merson, Martin. The Private Diary of a Public
        Servant. New York: Macmillan, 1955.

1278.   Nevins, Allan. Herbert H. Lehman and His Era.
        New York: Scribner, 1963.

1279.   Polsby, Nelson W. , "Towards an Explanation of
        McCarthyism, " Political Studies, VIII (October, 1960),
250-271.

1280.   Potter, Charles E. , Days of Shame. New York:
        Coward-McCann, 1965.

1281.   Rogin, Michael P. The Intellectuals and McCarthy:
        The Radical Specter. Cambridge: M.I.T. Press,
1967.

1282.   Rorty, James and Decter, Moshe. McCarthy and the
        Communists. Boston: Beacon Press, 1954.

1283.   Rovere, Richard H. Senator Joe McCarthy. New
        York: Harcourt, Brace, 1959.

1284.   Rubin, Morris, "McCarthy: A Documented Record, "
        Progressive, XVIII (April, 1954), 1-94.

1285.   Straight, Michael. Trial by Television. Boston:
        Beacon Press, 1954.

1286.   Thelen, David P. and Thelen, Esther S. , "Joe Must
        Go: The Movement to Recall Senator Joseph R.
McCarthy, " Wisconsin Magazine of History, XLIX (Spring,
1966), 185-209.

1287.   Trow, Martin, "Small Businessmen, Political
        Tolerance and Support for McCarthy, " American
Journal of Sociology, LXIV (November, 1958), 270-281.

1288.   U.S. Congress. Senate. Committee on Government
        Operations. Communist Infiltration among Army
Civilian Workers. Hearings before the Permanent Subcommittee on Government Operations ... Washington: Government Printing Office, 1953. (83d Congress, 1st Sess.)

1289.   _____. _____. Select Committee to Study
        Censure Charges. Report on Resolution to Censure.
Washington: Government Printing Office, 1954. (83d Cong. ,

2d Sess. Senate Report 2508). [Serial No. 11732].

1290. Varney, Harold Lloyd, "What Has Joe McCarthy
       Accomplished?" American Mercury, LXXVIII (May,
1954), 3-14.

1291. Wiebe, G. D. "The Army-McCarthy Hearings and
       the Public Conscience," Public Opinion Quarterly,
XXII (Winter 1958-59), 490-502.

1292. Wittenberg, Philip. The Lamont Case: History of a
       Congressional Investigation. New York: Horizon
Press, 1957.

1293. Wrong, Dennis, "Theories of McCarthyism--A Survey,"
       Dissent, I (Autumn, 1954), 385-392.

5. The Oppenheimer Security Case

1294. Alsop, Joseph and Alsop, Stewart. We Accuse! The
       Story of the Miscarriage of American Justice in the
Case of J. Robert Oppenheimer. New York: Simon and
Schuster, 1954.

1295. _____. _____, "We Accuse!" Harper's
       Magazine, CCIX (October, 1954), 25-45. Discussion
CCIX (October, 1954), 14-17; (December, 1954), 7-8.

1296. Chevalier, Haakon. Oppenheimer: The Story of a
       Friendship. New York: Braziller, 1965.

1297. Curtis, Charles P. The Oppenheimer Case: The
       Trial of a Security System. New York: Simon &
Schuster, 1955.

1298. Davis, Nuel Pharr. Lawrence and Oppenheimer.
       New York: Simon and Schuster, 1968.

1299. Hewlett, Richard G. and Duncan, Francis. Atomic
       Shield, 1947/1952 (A History of the United States
Atomic Energy Commission, v. 2). University Park: Pennsylvania State University Press, 1969.

1300. Jungk, Robert. Brighter than a Thousand Suns: A
       Personal History of the Atomic Scientists. New York:
Harcourt, Brace, 1958.

1301.   Kalven, Harry, "The Case of J. Robert Oppenheimer
          before the Atomic Energy Commission," Bulletin of the
Atomic Scientists, X (September, 1954), 259-269.

1302.   Kipphardt, Heinar.   In the Matter of J. Robert
          Oppenheimer: A Play.   New York: Hill and Wang,
1969c1968.

1303.   Lilienthal, David E.   The Journals of David E.
          Lilienthal.   New York: Harper & Row, 1964-1971.
5 vols.   Vol. III.

1304.   Michelmore, Peter.   The Swift Years: The Robert
          Oppenheimer Story.   New York: Dodd, Mead, 1969.

1305.   "New Debate on the Oppenheimer Case," U.S. News
          and World Report, XXXVII (December 24, 1954), 86-
103.   Reply to the Alsops' charges in We Accuse;   also their
rejoinder.

1306.   Rouzé, Michel.   Robert Oppenheimer: The Man and
          His Theories.   New York: P. S. Eriksson, 1965c1962.

1307.   Schlesinger, Arthur M., "The Oppenheimer Case,"
          Atlantic Monthly, CXCIV (October, 1954), 29-36.
Discussion CXCIV (December, 1954), 21-22.

1308.   Stern, Philip M. and Green, Harold P.   The Oppen-
          heimer Case: Security on Trial.   New York: Harper
& Row, 1969.

1309.   Strauss, Lewis L.   Men and Decisions.   Garden City:
          Doubleday, 1962.

1310.   Strout, Cushing, ed.   Conscience, Science and
          Security: The Case of Dr. J. Robert Oppenheimer.
Chicago: Rand McNally, 1963.

1311.   _____.   "Oppenheimer Case: Melodrama, Tragedy
          and Irony," Virginia Quarterly Review, XL (Spring,
1964), 268-280.

1312.   Trilling, Diana, "The Oppenheimer Case: A Reading
          of the Testimony," Partisan Review, XXI (November,
1954), 604-635.   Reply with rejoinder, H. Meyerhoff,
Partisan Review, XXII (Spring, 1955), 238-251.

1313. U.S. Atomic Energy Commission. In the Matter of
       J. Robert Oppenheimer. Washington: Government
Printing Office, 1954.

1314. _____. In the Matter of J. Robert Oppenheimer.
       Texts of Principal Documents and Letters. Washing-
ton: Government Printing Office, 1954.

1315. Wharton, Michael, ed. A Nation's Security: The
       Case of Dr. J. Robert Oppenheimer. Ed. from the
official transcript of evidence given before the Personnel
Security Board of the United States Atomic Energy Commission. London: Secker & Warburg, 1955.

1316. Wilson, Thomas W. The Great Weapons Heresy.
       Boston: Houghton Mifflin, 1970.

6. Espionage

1317. Dallin, David J. Soviet Espionage. New Haven:
       Yale University Press, 1955.

1318. De Toledano, Ralph. The Greatest Plot in History:
       How the Reds Stole the A-Bomb. New York: Duell,
Sloan and Pearce, 1963.

1319. Dulles, Allen. The Craft of Intelligence. New York:
       Harper & Row, 1963.

1320. Fiedler, Leslie A. An End to Innocence: Essays on
       Culture and Politics. Boston: Beacon Press, 1955.

1321. Fineberg, Solomon Andhil. The Rosenberg Case:
       Fact and Fiction. New York: Oceana Publications,
1953.

1322. Hilsman, Roger. Strategic Intelligence and National
       Decisions. Glencoe, Ill., Free Press, 1956.

1323. Kirkpatrick, Lyman B. The Real CIA. New York:
       Macmillan, 1968.

1324. Pilat, Oliver. The Atom Spies. New York: Putnam's,
       1952.

1325. Ransom, Harry Howe. Central Intelligence and

National Security. Cambridge: Harvard University
Press, 1958.

1326. _____. The Intelligence Establishment. Cambridge: Harvard University Press, 1970.

1327. Root, Jonathan. The Betrayers: The Rosenberg Case--
A Reappraisal of an American Crisis. New York:
Coward-McCann, 1963.

1328. Rourke, Francis E. Secrecy and Publicity: Dilemmas
of Democracy. Baltimore: Johns Hopkins Press, 1961.

1329. Schneir, Walter and Schneir, Miriam. Invitation to an
Inquest. New York: Doubleday, 1965.

1330. Tully, Andrew. CIA: The Inside Story. New York:
Morrow, 1962.

1331. Wexley, John. The Judgment of Julius and Ethel
Rosenberg. New York: Cameron & Kahn, 1955.

1332. Wise, David and Ross, Thomas B. The Invisible
Government. New York: Random House, 1964.

B.   CIVIL LIBERTIES AND CIVIL RIGHTS

1. General

1333. Abraham, Henry Julian. Freedom and the Court:
Civil Rights and Liberties in the United States. New
York: Oxford University Press, 1967.

1334. Abrams, Charles. Forbidden Neighbors: A Study
of Prejudice in Housing. New York: Harper, 1955.

1335. American Civil Liberties Union. Report, 1945/46 -
1960/61. New York: American Civil Liberties
Union, 1946-1961.

1336. Anderson, John Weir. Eisenhower, Brownell, and
the Congress: The Tangled Origins of the Civil Rights
Bill of 1956-1957. University, Ala.: University of Alabama
Press, 1964.

1337. Arnold, Thurman. Fair Fights and Foul: A Dissenting

Lawyer's Life. New York: Harcourt, Brace, 1965.

1338.   Bartley, Numan V.   The Rise of Massive Resistance:
        Race and Politics in the South During the 1950's.
Baton Rouge: Louisiana State University Press, 1969.

1339.   Berger, Morroe.   Equality by Statute: Legal Controls
        over Group Discrimination.   New York: Columbia
University Press, 1952.

1340.   _____.   Equality by Statute: The Revolution in
        Civil Rights.   Rev. ed.   Garden City: Doubleday,
1967.

1341.   Berman, Daniel M.   A Bill Becomes a Law: The
        Civil Rights Act of 1960.   New York: Macmillan,
1962.

1342.   Berman, William C.   The Politics of Civil Rights
        in the Truman Administration.   Columbus: Ohio
State University Press, 1970.

1343.   Biddle, Francis B.   The Fear of Freedom: A Dis-
        cussion of the Contemporary Obsession of Anxiety
and Fear in the United States.   Garden City: Doubleday,
1951.

1344.   Carr, Robert K. , ed. , "Civil Rights in America,"
        American Academy of Political and Social Science.
Annals, CCLXXV (May, 1951), 1-161.

1345.   _____.   The Federal Protection of Civil Rights:
        Quest for a Sword.   Ithaca: Cornell University Press,
1947.

1346.   Caughey, John W.   In Clear and Present Danger:
        The Crucial State of Our Freedoms.   Chicago: Uni-
versity of Chicago Press, 1958.

1347.   Chafee, Zechariah.   The Blessings of Liberty.
        Philadelphia: Lippincott, 1956.

1348.   Clark, Tom C. and Perlman, Philip B.   Prejudice
        and Property: An Historic Brief against Racial Cov-
enants Submitted to the Supreme Court ...   Washington:
Public Affairs Press, 1948.

1349. Commager, Henry Steele. Freedom, Loyalty, Dissent.
       New York: Oxford University Press, 1954.

1350. Commission on Freedom of the Press. Freedom of
       the Press: A Framework of Principle by W. E.
Hocking [and other members of the Commission]. Chicago:
University of Chicago Press, 1947.

1351. _____. Government and Mass Communications, a
       Report by Zechariah Chafee. Chicago: University
of Chicago Press, 1947. 2 vols.

1352. Cushman, Robert E. Civil Liberties in the United
       States: A Guide to Current Problems and Experience.
Ithaca: Cornell University Press, 1956.

1353. Davis, Elmer. But We Were Born Free. Indianap-
       olis: Bobbs-Merrill, 1954.

1354. Davis, Jerome. Character Assassination. New
       York: Philosophical Library, 1950.

1355. Divine, Robert A. American Immigration Policy,
       1924-1952. New Haven: Yale University Press,
1957.

1356. Dulles, Foster Rhea. The Civil Rights Commission,
       1957-1965. East Lansing: Michigan State University
Press, 1968.

1357. Ernst, Morris L. The First Freedom. New York:
       Macmillan, 1946.

1358. Faulk, John Henry. Fear on Trial. New York:
       Simon & Schuster, 1964.

1359. Fellman, David. The Limits of Freedom. New
       Brunswick, N. J. : Rutgers University Press, 1959.
(Brown and Haley Lectures, University of Puget Sound).

1360. Forster, Arnold and Epstein, Benjamin R. The
       Troublemakers: An Anti-Defamation League Report.
Garden City: Doubleday, 1952.

1361. Fraenkel, Osmond K. The Supreme Court and Civil
       Liberties: How the Court Has Protected the Bill of
Rights. 2d ed. Dobbs Ferry, N. Y. : Published for the

American Civil Liberties Union by Oceana Publications, 1963.

1362.   Grimes, Alan P.   Equality in America: Religion,
        Race, and the Urban Majority.   New York: Oxford
University Press, 1964.

1363.   Handlin, Oscar.   Fire-Bell in the Night: The Crisis
        in Civil Rights.   Boston: Little, Brown, 1964.

1364.   Harris, Robert J.   The Quest for Equality: The
        Constitution, Congress, and the Supreme Court.
Baton Rouge: Louisiana State University Press, 1960.

1365.   Kalven, Harry.   The Negro and the First Amendment.
        Columbus: Ohio State University Press, 1965.

1366.   Kelly, Alfred H.   Foundations of Freedom in the
        American Constitution.   New York: Harper, 1958.

1367.   Kemper, Donald J.   Decade of Fear: Senator Hennings
        and Civil Liberties.   Columbia: University of Mis-
souri Press, 1965.

1368.   King, Martin Luther.   Stride toward Freedom: The
        Montgomery Story.   New York: Harper & Row, 1958.

1369.   Konvitz, Milton R.   Civil Rights in Immigration.
        Ithaca: Cornell University Press, 1953.

1370.   _____.   Expanding Liberties: Freedom's Gains in
        Postwar America.   New York: Viking Press, 1966.

1371.   Lamont, Corliss.   Freedom Is As Freedom Does:
        Civil Liberties Today.   New York: Horizon Press,
1956.

1372.   Lasswell, Harold D.   National Security and Individual
        Freedom.   New York: McGraw-Hill, 1950.

1373.   Lewis, Anthony and the New York Times.   Portrait
        of a Decade: The Second American Revolution.   New
York: Random House, 1964.

1374.   Lomax, Louis E.   The Negro Revolt.   New York:
        Harper, 1962.

1375.   Longaker, Richard P.   The Presidency and Individual

Liberties. Ithaca: Cornell University Press, 1961.

1376. McCain, R. Ray, "Reactions to the United States
       Supreme Court Decision of 1954," Georgia Historical
Quarterly, LII (December, 1968), 371-387.

1377. McCoy, Donald R. and Ruetten, Richard T., "The
       Civil Rights Movement, 1940-1954. Midwest Quarterly.
XI (October, 1969), 11-34.

1378. MacIver, Robert. Academic Freedom in Our Time.
       New York: Columbia University Press, 1955.

1379. Moon, Henry Lee. Balance of Power: The Negro
       Vote. Garden City: Doubleday, 1948.

1380. O'Brian, John Lord. National Security and Individual
       Freedom. Cambridge: Harvard University Press,
1955.

1381. _____, "New Encroachments on Individual Freedom,"
       Harvard Law Review, LXVI (November, 1952), 1-27.

1382. Pritchett, C. Herman. Civil Liberties and the Vinson
       Court. Chicago: University of Chicago Press, 1954.

1383. Rogge, Oetje John. Our Vanishing Civil Liberties.
       New York: Gaer Associates, 1949.

1384. Schwartz, Bernard. Civil Rights. New York:
       Chelsea House in association with McGraw-Hill,
1970. 2 vols. (Statutory History of the United States).

1385. Spinrad, William. Civil Liberties. Chicago:
       Quadrangle Books. 1970.

1386. Stouffer, Samuel A. Communism, Conformity, and
       Civil Liberties. Garden City: Doubleday, 1955.

1387. Thomas, Norman M. The Test of Freedom. New
       York: Norton, 1954.

1388. Truman, Harry S. Freedom and Equality: Addresses.
       Ed. by David Horton. Columbia: University of Mis-
souri Press, 1960.

1389. U.S. President's Committee on Civil Rights. To

Secure These Rights: The Report of the President's Committee on Civil Rights. Washington: Government Printing Office, 1947. Also New York: Simon & Schuster, 1947.

1390. Weintraub, Ruth G. How Secure These Rights? Anti-Semitism in the United States in 1948: An Anti-Defamation League Survey. Garden City: Doubleday, 1949.

1391. White, Walter F. How Far the Promised Land. New York: Viking Press, 1955.

1392. _____. A Man Called White: The Autobiography of Walter White. New York: Viking Press, 1948.

1393. Wilcox, Clair, ed. Civil Liberties under Attack. Philadelphia: University of Pennsylvania Press, 1951.

1394. Woodward, Comer Vann. The Strange Career of Jim Crow. 2d rev. ed. New York: Oxford University Press, 1966.

2. Race Relations

    a. General

1395. Ashmore, Harry. The Negro and the Schools. 2d ed. Chapel Hill: University of North Carolina Press, 1954. Originally published on May 16, 1954. The text of the Supreme Court decision of May 17 appears in the second edition.

1396. Baldwin, James. Nobody Knows My Name: More Notes of a Native Son. New York: Dial Press, 1961.

1397. _____. Notes of a Native Son. New York: Dial Press, 1955.

1398. Bolner, James, "Mr. Chief Justice Fred M. Vinson and Racial Discrimination," Register of the Kentucky Historical Society, LXIV (January, 1966), 29-43.

1399. Conrad, Earl. Jim Crow America. New York: Duell, Sloan and Pearce, 1947.

1400. Essien-Udom, Essien Udosen. Black Nationalism: A Search for an Identity in America. Chicago:

University of Chicago Press, 1962.

1401.   Frazier, Edward Franklin. Black Bourgeoisie. New
        York: Free Press, 1957.

1402.   Glazer, Nathan and Moynihan, Daniel P. Beyond the
        Melting Pot: The Negroes, Puerto Ricans, Jews,
Italians, and Irish of New York City. Cambridge: M. I. T.
Press and Harvard University Press, 1963.

1403.   Greenberg, Jack. Race Relations and American Law.
        New York: Columbia University Press, 1959.

1404.   Kalven, Harry. The Negro and the First Amendment.
        Columbus: Ohio State University Press, 1965.

1405.   King, Martin Luther. Stride toward Freedom: The
        Montgomery Story. New York: Harper & Row, 1958.

1406.   Lincoln, Charles Eric. The Black Muslims in
        America. Boston: Beacon Press, 1961.

1407.   Lomax, Louis E. The Negro Revolt. New York:
        Harper & Row, 1962.

1408.   Newby, Idus A. Challenge to the Court: Social
        Scientists and the Defense of Segregation, 1954-1966.
Rev. ed. Baton Rouge: Louisiana State University Press,
1969.

1409.   Record, Wilson. The Negro and the Communist
        Party. Chapel Hill: University of North Carolina
Press, 1951.

1410.   Rowan, Carl Thomas. South of Freedom. New York:
        Knopf, 1952.

1411.   Smith, Frank E. Congressman from Mississippi.
        New York: Pantheon Books, 1964.

1412.   White, Walter F. A Man Called White: The Auto-
        biography of Walter White.

1413.   Woodward, Comer Vann. The Strange Career of Jim
        Crow. 2d rev. ed. New York: Oxford University
Press, 1966.

b.   Military Desegregation

1414.   Billington, Monroe, "Freedom to Serve: The Presi-
         dent's Committee on Equality of Treatment and
Opportunity in the Armed Forces, 1949-1950," Journal of
Negro History, LI (October, 1966), 262-274.

1415.   Bogart, Leo, ed.   Social Research and the Desegre-
         gation of the U. S. Army: Two Original 1951 Field
Reports by Leo Bogart and others.   Chicago: Markham
Publishing Company, 1969.

1416.   Dalfiume, Richard M.   Desegregation of the U. S.
         Armed Forces: Fighting on Two Fronts, 1939-1953.
Columbia: University of Missouri Press, 1969.

1417.   Mandelbaum, David Goodman.   Soldier Groups and
         Negro Soldiers.   Berkeley: University of California
Press, 1952.

1418.   Nichols, Lee.   Breakthrough on the Color Front.
         New York: Random House, 1954.

1419.   Paszek, Lawrence J. , "Negroes and the Air Force,
         1939-1949," Military Affairs, XXXI (Spring, 1967),
1-9.

1420.   Reddick, L. D. , "The Negro Policy of the American
         Army Since World War II," Journal of Negro History,
XXXVIII (April, 1953), 196-215.

1421.   Stillman, Richard J.   Integration of the Negro in the
         U. S. Armed Forces.   New York: Praeger, 1968.

1422.   U. S. President's Committee on Equality of Treatment
         and Opportunity in the Armed Services.   Freedom to
Serve: A Report by the President's Committee.   Washington:
Government Printing Office, 1950.

c.   School Desegregation

1423.   Ashmore, Harry.   The Negro and the Schools.   2d
         ed.   Chapel Hill: University of North Carolina Press,
1954.   First published May 16, 1954.   On May 17 the Supreme Court handed down its famous decision, the text of
which appears in the second edition.

1424.   Bartley, Numan V. , "Looking Back at Little Rock,"
         Arkansas Historical Quarterly, XXV (Summer, 1966),
101-116.

1425.   Bates, Daisy Gatson.   The Long Shadow of Little
         Rock: A Memoir.   New York: McKay, 1962.

1426.   Berman, Daniel M.   It Is So Ordered: The Supreme
         Court Rules on School Desegregation.   New York:
Norton, 1966.

1427.   Blaustein, Albert P. and Ferguson, Clarence C.
         Desegregation and the Law: The Meaning and Effect
of the School Segregation Cases.   2d rev. ed.   New York:
Vintage Books, 1962.   First published 1957 New Brunswick,
N. J. , Rutgers University Press.

1428.   Brown, Oliver.   Argument: Argument: The Oral
         Argument before the Supreme Court in Brown v.
Board of Education of Topeka, 1952-55.   New York: Chelsea
House, 1969.

1429.   Gates, Robbins L.   The Making of Massive Resistance:
         Virginia's Politics of Public School Desegregation,
1954-1956.   Chapel Hill: University of North Carolina Press,
1965.

1430.   Martin, John B.   The Deep South Says Never.   New
         York: Ballantine Books, 1957.

1431.   Muse, Benjamin.   Ten Years of Prelude: The Story
         of Integration Since the Supreme Court's 1954 Decision.
New York: Viking Press, 1964.

1432.   _____.   Virginia's Massive Resistance.   Blooming-
         ton: Indiana University Press, 1961.

1433.   Shoemaker, Don, ed.   With All Deliberate Speed:
         Segregation-Desegregation in Southern Schools.   New
York: Harper, 1957.

1434.   Smith, Bob (Robert Collins).   They Closed Their
         Schools: Prince Edward County, Virginia, 1951-1964.
Chapel Hill: University of North Carolina Press, 1965.

C. THE AMERICAN ECONOMY

1. Agricultural Policy

1435. Benedict, Murray R. and Stine, Oscar Clemen. The
       Agricultural Commodity Programs: Two Decades of
Experience. New York: Twentieth Century Fund, 1956.

1436. _____. Can We Solve the Farm Problem? An
       Analysis of Federal Aid to Agriculture. New York:
Twentieth Century Fund, 1955.

1437. _____. Farm Policies of the United States: A
       Study of Their Origins and Development. New York:
Twentieth Century Fund, 1953.

1438. _____. and Bauer, Elizabeth Kelley. Farm Sur-
       pluses: U. S. , Burden or Asset? Berkeley: University
of California. Division of Agricultural Sciences, 1960.

1439. Benson, Ezra T. Cross Fire: The Eight Years with
       Eisenhower. Garden City: Doubleday, 1962.

1440. Bernstein, Barton J. , "Clash of Interests: The Post-
       war Battle between the Office of Price Administration
and Agriculture," Agricultural History, XLI (January, 1967),
45-57.

1441. _____. , "The Postwar Famine and Price Control,
       1946," Agricultural History, XXXVIII (October, 1964),
235-240.

1442. Block, William J. The Separation of the Farm Bureau
       and the Extension Service: Political Issue in a Federal
System. Urbana: University of Illinois Press, 1960. (Illinois Studies in the Social Sciences, Vol. 47).

1443. Christenson, Reo M. The Brannan Plan: Farm
       Politics and Policy. Ann Arbor: University of
Michigan Press, 1959.

1444. Crampton, John A. The National Farmers Union:
       Ideology of a Pressure Group. Lincoln: University
of Nebraska Press, 1965.

1445. Hardin, Charles M. , "Farm Policy and the Farm
       Vote," Journal of Farm Economics, (November, 1955),
601-624.

1446. _____. The Politics of Agriculture: Soil Conser-
       vation and the Struggle for Power in Rural America.
Glencoe, Ill.:   Free Press, 1952.

1447. Hathaway, Dale E. Government and Agriculture:
       Public Policy in a Democratic Society. New York:
Macmillan, 1963.

1448. Hickman, Charles Addison. Our Farm Program and
       Foreign Trade: A Conflict of National Policies. New
York: Council on Foreign Relations, 1949.

1449. Johnson, David Gale. Trade and Agriculture: A
       Study of Inconsistent Policies. New York: Wiley,
1950.

1450. McConnell, Grant. The Decline of Agrarian Democ-
       racy. Berkeley: University of California Press,
1953.

1451. Matusow, Allen J. Farm Policies and Politics in
       the Truman Years. Cambridge: Harvard University
Press, 1967.

1452. Paarlberg, Donald. American Farm Policy: A Case
       of Centralized Decision Making. New York: Wiley,
1964.

1453. Ruttan, Vernon W., Waldo, Arley D., and Houck,
       James P. Agricultural Policy in an Affluent Society.
New York: Norton, 1969.

1454. Schoff, Leonard Hastings. A National Agricultural
       Policy for All the People of the United States. New
York: Harper, 1950.

1455. Schultz, Theodore William. Agriculture in an Unstable
       Economy. New York: McGraw-Hill, 1945.

1456. Williams, Oliver P., "The Commodity Credit Corpor-
       ation and the 1948 Presidential Election," Midwest
Journal of Political Science, I (August, 1957), 111-124.

2. Economic Conditions

1457. Adelman, M. A., "The Measurement of Industrial
       Concentration," Review of Economics and Statistics,

XXXIII (November, 1951), 269-296.

1458.   Baran, Paul A. , and Sweezy, Paul M.   Monopoly
        Capital: An Essay on the American Economic and
Social Order.   New York: Monthly Review Press, 1966.

1459.   _____.   The Political Economy of Growth.   New
        York: Monthly Review Press, 1957.

1460.   Bator, Francis M.   The Question of Government
        Spending: Public Needs and Private Wants.   New
York: Harper, 1960.

1461.   Berle, Adolph A.   The Twentieth Century Capitalist
        Revolution.   New York: Harcourt, Brace & World,
1954.

1462.   Bernstein, Barton J. , "The Removal of War Produc-
        tion Controls on Business, 1944-1946," Business
History Review, XXXIX (Summer, 1965), 243-260.

1463.   Bidwell, Percy Wells.   Raw Materials: A Study of
        American Policy.   New York: Published for the
Council on Foreign Relations by Harper, 1958.

1464.   Blyth, Conrad A.   American Business Cycles, 1945-
        50.   New York: Praeger, 1969.

1465.   Bronfenbrenner, Martin, "Postwar Political Economy:
        The President's Reports," Journal of Political Econ-
omy, LVI (October, 1948), 373-391.

1466.   Butters, John Keith, Thompson, Lawrence E. and
        Bollinger, Lynn L.   Effects of Taxation: Investments
by Individuals.   Boston: Division of Research, Graduate
School of Business Administration, Harvard University, 1953.

1467.   Chandler, Lester V.   Inflation in the United States,
        1940-1948.   New York: Harper, 1951.

1468.   Clark, John Maurice.   Guideposts in Time of Change.
        New York: Harper, 1949.

1469.   Coit, Margaret L.   Mr. Baruch.   Boston: Houghton
        Mifflin, 1957.

1470.   Dewhurst, James Frederic and others.   America's

Needs and Resources. New York: Twentieth Century Fund, 1955.

1471. Drucker, Peter F. The New Society: The Anatomy of the Industrial Order. New York: Harper, 1950.

1472. Eccles, Marriner. Beckoning Frontiers: Public and Personal Recollections. Ed. by Sidney Human. New York: Knopf, 1951.

1473. Freeman, Ralph E. , ed. Postwar Economic Trends in the United States. New York: Harper, 1960.

1474. Galbraith, John Kenneth. The Affluent Society. 2d ed. rev. Boston: Houghton Mifflin, 1969. First published 1958.

1475. _____, "The Affluent Society After Ten Years," Atlantic, CCXXIII (May, 1969), 37-44.

1476. _____. American Capitalism: The Concept of Countervailing Power. Rev. ed. Boston: Houghton Mifflin, 1956.

1477. _____. The New Industrial State. Boston: Houghton Mifflin, 1967.

1478. _____. A Theory of Price Control. Cambridge: Harvard University Press, 1952.

1479. Goldsmith, Raymond William. The National Wealth of the United States in the Post-War Period. Princeton: Princeton University Press, 1962. (National Bureau of Economic Research. Studies in Capital Formation and Financing, 10).

1480. Gross, Bertram M. and Lewis, John Prior, "The President's Economic Staff During the Truman Administration," American Political Science Review, XLVIII (March, 1954), 114-130.

1481. Hacker, Andrew, ed. The Corporation Take-Over. New York: Harper & Row, 1964.

1482. Hagen, Everett E. , "The Reconversion Period: Reflections of Forecaster," Review of Economics and Statistics, XXIX (May, 1947), 95-101.

1483.   Hardt, John Pearce, Stolzenbach, C. Darwin and
        Kohn, Martin J.   The Cold War Economic Gap: The
Increasing Threat to American Supremacy.   New York:
Praeger, 1961.

1484.   Harris, Seymour Edwin, ed.   Economic Reconstruc-
        tion.   New York: McGraw-Hill, 1945.

1485.   Hickman, Bert G.   Growth and Stability of the Post-
        war Economy.   Washington: Brookings Institution,
1960.

1486.   Holmans, A. E. , "The Eisenhower Administration
        and the Recession, 1953-1955," Oxford Economic
Papers, n. s. X (February, 1958), 34-54.

1487.   Kaplan, Abraham D. H.   Big Enterprise in a Com-
        petitive System.   Washington: Brookings Institution,
1954.

1488.   Katona, George and Mueller, Eva.   Consumer Atti-
        tudes and Demand, 1950-1952.   Ann Arbor: Survey
Research Center, Institute for Social Research, University
of Michigan, 1953.

1489.   _____.   The Mass Consumption Society.   New
        York: McGraw-Hill, 1964.

1490.   Keezer, Dexter Merriam and others.   Making
        Capitalism Work: A Program for Preserving Freedom
and Stabilizing Prosperity.   New York: McGraw-Hill, 1950.

1491.   Kolko, Gabriel.   Wealth and Power in America: An
        Analysis of Social Class and Income Distribution.
New York: Praeger, 1962.

1492.   Koot, Ronald S. and Walker, David A. , "Economic
        Growth and Stability Since the Employment Act of
1946," Quarterly Review of Economics and Business, X
(Autumn, 1970), 7-17.

1493.   Kuznets, Simon Smith and Jenks, Elizabeth.   Capital
        in the American Economy: Its Formation and Financing.
Princeton: Princeton University Press, 1961.   (National
Bureau of Economic Research.   Studies).

1494.   Lampman, Robert J.   The Share of the Top Wealth-

Holders in National Wealth, 1922-1956. Princeton:
Princeton University Press, 1962. (National Bureau of
Economic Research. Studies).

1495. Lee, R. Alton, "Federal Assistance in Depressed
      Areas in the Postwar Recession," Western Economic
Journal, II (Fall, 1963), 1-23.

1496. Lekachman, Robert. The Age of Keynes. New York:
      Random House, 1966.

1497. Lilienthal, David E. Big Business: A New Era. New
      York: Harper, 1953.

1498. Mason, Edward S. , ed. The Corporation in Modern
      Society. Cambridge: Harvard University Press, 1960.

1499. _____. Economic Concentration and the Monopoly
      Problem. Cambridge: Harvard University Press,
1959. (Harvard Economic Studies Vol. 100).

1500. Means, Gardiner C. The Corporate Revolution in
      America: Economic Reality vs. Economic Theory.
New York: Crowell-Collier Press, 1962.

1501. _____. Pricing Power & the Public Interest: A
      Study Based on Steel. New York: Harper & Row,
1962.

1502. Melman, Seymour. Our Depleted Society. New
      York: Holt, Rinehart and Winston, 1965.

1503. Miller, Herman P. Rich Man, Poor Man. New
      York: Crowell, 1964.

1504. Myrdal, Gunnar. Challenge to Affluence. New York:
      Pantheon Books, 1963.

1505. Packer, Herbert L. The State of Research in Anti-
      Trust Law. New Haven: Walter E. Meyer Institute
of Law, 1963.

1506. Perlo, Victor, "People's Capitalism and Stock Owner-
      ship," American Economic Review, XLVIII (June,
1958), 333-347.

1507. Reder, Melvin W. , "The General Level of Money

Wages," Industrial Relations Research Proceedings, III (December, 1950), 186-202.

1508.   Sapir, Michael, "Review of Economic Forecasts for the Transition Period," with comment by Lawrence Klein and others.   Studies in Income and Wealth, Vol. XI, 1949, p. 273-367.

1509.   "Ten Economists on the Inflation," Review of Economics and Statistics, XXX (February, 1948), 1-29.

1510.   U. S. Congress.   Joint Economic Committee.   Employment, Growth and Price Levels, Hearings.   Washington: Government Printing Office, 1959-60.   10 parts in 14 vols.   (86th Cong. , 2d Sess.)

1511.   _____ .   _____ .   Relationship of Prices to Economic Stability and Growth: Hearings.   Washington: Government Printing Office, 1958-1959.   3 vols.   (85th Cong. , 2d Sess.)

1512.   Woytinsky, Wladimir S. , "What Was Wrong in Forecasts of Postwar Depression?"   Journal of Political Economy, LV (April, 1947), 142-151.

3.   Economic Policy

1513.   Abels, Jules.   The Welfare State: A Mortgage on America's Future.   New York: Duell, Sloan and Pearce, 1951.

1514.   Bernstein, Barton J. , "Reluctance and Resistance: Wilson Wyatt and Veterans' Housing in the Truman Administration," Register of the Kentucky Historical Society, LXV (January, 1967), 47-66.

1515.   Broude, Henry W.   Steel Decisions and the National Economy.   New Haven: Yale University Press, 1963.   (Yale Studies in Economics, 16).

1516.   Burns, Arthur F.   The Business Cycle in a Changing World.   New York: National Bureau of Economic Research, 1969.   Distributed by Columbia University Press.   (Studies in Business Cycles, 17).

1517.   _____ .   The Frontiers of Economic Knowledge: Essays.   Princeton: Published for the National

Bureau of Economic Research by Princeton University Press, 1954.

1518. _____. and Samuelson, Paul A. Full Employment:
        Guideposts and Economic Stability. Washington:
American Enterprise Institute for Public Policy Research, 1967.

1519. _____. The Management of Prosperity. New
        York: Distributed by Columbia University Press,
1966.

1520. _____. Prosperity without Inflation. New York:
        Fordham University Press, 1957. Buffalo: Smith,
Keynes & Marshall, distributed by Doubleday, Garden City,
1958.

1521. Bursk, Edward C. , ed. Thinking Ahead for Business.
        Cambridge: Harvard University Press, 1952.

1522. Childs, Marquis W. and Cater, Douglass. Ethics in
        a Business Society. New York: Harper, 1954.

1523. Crosser, Paul K. State Capitalism in the Economy
        of the United States. New York: Bookman Associates,
1960.

1524. Dale, Edwin L. Conservatives in Power: A Study
        in Frustration. Garden City: Doubleday, 1960.

1525. Davies, Richard O. , " 'Mr. Republican' Turns
        'Socialist': Robert A. Taft and Public Housing,"
Ohio History, LXXIII (Summer, 1964), 135-143.

1526. _____. Housing Reform During the Truman
        Administration. Columbia: University of Missouri
Press, 1966.

1527. Edwards, Corwin D. The Price Discrimination Law:
        A Review of Experience. Washington: Brookings
Institution, 1959.

1528. Fertig, Lawrence. Prosperity through Freedom.
        Chicago: Regnery, 1961.

1529. Foy, Bernard L. , "Dixon-Yates Data," Library
        Journal, LXXX (May 1, 1955), 1055-1056.

1530. Galbraith, John Kenneth. Economics & the Art of
       Controversy. New Brunswick, N. J. , Rutgers Univer-
sity Press, 1955. (Brown and Haley Lectures, University of
Puget Sound, 1954).

1531. Glueck, Sheldon, ed. The Welfare State and the
       National Welfare: A Symposium on Some of the
Threatening Tendencies of Our Times. Cambridge: Addison-
Wesley Press, 1952.

1532. Hansen, Alvin H. Economic Issues of the 1960's.
       New York: McGraw-Hill, 1960.

1533. Hansen, Alvin H. Economic Policy and Full Employ-
       ment. New York: McGraw-Hill, 1947.

1534. Harris, Seymour Edwin, ed. Foreign Economic
       Policy for the United States. Cambridge: Harvard
University Press, 1948.

1535. _____. The Economics of the Political Parties:
       With Special Attention to Presidents Eisenhower and
Kennedy. New York: Macmillan, 1962.

1536. _____, ed. Saving American Capitalism: A
       Liberal Economic Program. New York: Knopf,
1948.

1537. Hauge, Gabriel, "Economics of Eisenhower Dynamic
       Conservatism," Commercial and Financial Chronicle,
CLXXXII (October 27, 1955), 1749, 1776-1777.

1538. Hayek, Friedrich A. The Road to Serfdom. Chicago:
       University of Chicago Press, 1944.

1539. Jones, E. Terrence, "Congressional Voting on
       Keynesian Legislation, 1945-1964," Western Political
Quarterly, XXI (June, 1968), 240-251.

1540. Kaplan, Abraham D. H. , Dirlam, Joel B. and
       Lanzillotti, Robert F. Pricing in Big Business: A
Case Approach. Washington: Brookings Institution, 1958.

1541. Latham, Earl. The Group Basis of Politics: A
       Study of Basing-Point Legislation. Ithaca: Published
for Amherst College by Cornell University Press, 1962.

1542.   Leeman, Wayne A.   The Price of Middle East Oil:
         An Essay in Political Economy.   Ithaca: Cornell
University Press, 1962.

1543.   Machlup, Fritz.   The Basing-Point System: An
         Economic Analysis of a Controversial Pricing Prac-
tice.   Philadelphia: Blakiston, 1949.

1544.   Millett, John D.   The Process and Organization of
         Government Planning.   New York: Columbia Univer-
sity Press, 1947.

1545.   Morton, Walter A., "Keynesianism and Inflation,"
         Journal of Political Economy, LIX (June, 1951),
258-265.

1546.   Murphy, Charles J. V., "The Budget and Eisenhower,"
         Fortune, LVI (July, 1957), 96-99.

1547.   _____., "The Eisenhower Shift," Fortune, LIII
         (January, 1956), 82-87.

1548.   Nelson, Donald M.   Arsenal of Democracy: The
         Story of American War Production.   New York:
Harcourt, Brace, 1946.

1549.   Nelson, James Cecil.   Railroad Transportation and
         Public Policy.   Washington: Brookings Institution,
1959.

1550.   Nourse, Edwin G.   Economics in the Public Service:
         Administrative Aspects of the Employment Act.   New
York: Harcourt, Brace, 1953.

1551.   Penrose, Ernest.   Economic Planning for Peace.
         Princeton: Princeton University Press, 1953.

1552.   Randall, Clarence B.   A Foreign Economic Policy
         for the United States.   Chicago: University of
Chicago Press, 1954.

1553.   _____.   Freedom's Faith.   Boston: Little, Brown,
         1953.

1554.   Rostow, Eugene V.   Planning for Freedom: The
         Public Law of American Capitalism.   New Haven:
Yale University Press, 1959.

1555.   Schriftgiesser, Karl.   Business and Public Policy:
        The Role of the Committee for Economic Develop-
ment, 1942-1967.   Englewood Cliffs, N. J., Prentice-Hall,
1967.

1556.   _____.   Business Comes of Age: The Story of the
        Committee for Economic Development ... 1942-1960.
New York: Harper, 1960.

1557.   Schumpeter, Joseph A.   Capitalism, Socialism and
        Democracy.   3d ed.   New York: Harper, 1950.

1558.   Simons, Henry C.   Economic Policy for a Free
        Society.   Chicago: University of Chicago Press,
1948.

1559.   Slichter, Sumner Huber.   The American Economy:
        Its Problems and Prospects.   New York: Knopf,
1948.

1560.   Somers, Herman Miles.   Presidential Agency: OWMR,
        Office of War Mobilization and Reconversion.   Cam-
bridge: Harvard University Press, 1950.

1561.   Stassen, Harold E.   Man Was Meant to Be Free:
        Selected Statements, 1940-1951.   Garden City:
Doubleday, 1951.

1562.   Theobald, Robert.   The Challenge of Abundance.
        New York: C. N. Potter, 1961.

1563.   U. S. Commission on Foreign Economic Policy.
        Minority Report, by Daniel A. Reed and Richard M.
Simpson.   Washington: Government Printing Office, 1954.

1564.   _____.   Report to the President and the Congress.
        Washington: Government Printing Office, 1954.
Clarence B. Randall, Chairman.

1565.   Whitney, Simon N.   Antitrust Policies: American
        Experience in Twenty Industries.   New York:
Twentieth Century Fund, 1958.   2 vols.

1566.   Wildavsky, Aaron.   Dixon-Yates: A Study in Power
        Policies.   New Haven: Yale University Press, 1962.
(Yale Studies in Political Science, 3).

1567. Willoughby, William R. The St. Lawrence Waterway:
         A Study in Politics and Diplomacy. Madison: Uni-
versity of Wisconsin Press, 1961.

4. Fiscal Policy

1568. Abbott, Charles C. The Federal Debt, Structure and
         Impact. New York: Twentieth Century Fund, 1953.

1569. Ahearn, Daniel S. Federal Reserve Policy Re-
         appraised, 1951-1959. New York: Columbia Uni-
versity Press, 1963.

1570. Bach, George Leland. Federal Reserve Policy-
         Making: A Study in Government Economic Policy
Formation. New York: Knopf, 1950.

1571. Behrman, Jack N. , "Political Factors in U.S.
         International Financial Cooperation, 1945-1950,"
American Political Science Review, XLVII (June, 1953),
431-60.

1572. Chandler, Lester V. , "Federal Reserve Policy and
         the Federal Debt," American Economic Review,
XXXIX (March, 1949), 405-429.

1573. Copeland, Morris A. Trends in Government Financing.
         Princeton: Published for the National Bureau of
Economic Research by Princeton University Press, 1961.

1574. Douglas, Paul H. Economy in the National Govern-
         ment. Chicago: University of Chicago Press, 1952.

1575. Fenno, Richard F. The Power of the Purse: Ap-
         propriations Politics in Congress. Boston: Little,
Brown, 1966.

1576. Friedman, Milton and Schwartz, Anna J. A Monetary
         History of the United States, 1867-1960. Princeton:
Princeton University Press, 1963.

1577. Gardner, Richard N. Sterling-Dollar Diplomacy: The
         Origins and the Prospects of Our International Eco-
nomic Order. New and expanded ed. New York: McGraw-
Hill, 1969. First published 1956.

1578. Harris, Seymour Edwin, ed. , "The Controversy over

Monetary Policy," a series of seven articles. Review of Economics and Statistics, XXXIII (August, 1951), 179-200.

1579. Hart, Albert G. Defense and the Dollar: Federal Credit and Monetary Policy. New York: Twentieth Century Fund, 1953.

1580. _____. Defense without Inflation. New York: Twenteith Century Fund, 1951.

1581. _____. and Brown, E. Cary. Financing Defense. New York: Twentieth Century Fund, 1951.

1582. Holmans, A. E. United States Fiscal Policy, 1945-1959: Its Contribution to Economic Stability. London: Oxford University Press, 1961.

1583. Humphrey, George M. The Basic Papers of George M. Humphrey As Secretary of the Treasury, 1953-1957. Ed. by Nathaniel R. Howard. Cleveland: Western Reserve Historical Society. 1965.

1584. Jacoby, Neil Herman, ed. United States Monetary Policy: Its Contribution to Prosperity without Inflation. New York: American Assembly, 1958.

1585. Knipe, James L. The Federal Reserve and the American Dollar: Problems and Policies, 1946-1964. Chapel Hill: University of North Carolina Press, 1965.

1586. Lewis, Wilfred. Federal Fiscal Policy in the Postwar Recessions. Washington: Brookings Institution, 1962. (Studies of Government Finance, 1).

1587. Murphy, Henry C. The National Debt in War and Transition. New York: McGraw-Hill, 1950.

1588. Smithies, Arthur. The Budgetary Process in the United States. New York: McGraw-Hill, 1955.

1589. Stern, Philip M. The Great Treasury Raid. New York: Random House, 1964.

1590. Survey of United States International Finance, [v. 1] - [v. 5], 1949-1953, ed. by Gardner Patterson and Jack N. Behrman. Princeton: Princeton University Press, 1950-1954.

1591. U. S. Congress. Joint Economic Committee. Mone-
       tary Policy and the Management of the Public Debt.
Washington: Government Printing Office, 1952. 2 vols.
(82d Cong. , 2d Sess. Senate Document 123).

5. Business and Industry

1592. Adams, Walter and Gray, Horace M. Monopoly in
       America: The Government As Promoter. New York:
Macmillan, 1955.

1593. Bernstein, Marver H. Regulating Business by
       Independent Commission. Princeton: Princeton
University Press, 1955.

1594. Bunzel, John H. The American Small Businessman.
       New York: Knopf, 1962.

1595. Cassady, Ralph. Price Making and Price Behavior
       in the Petroleum Industry. New Haven: Yale Uni-
versity Press, 1954. (Petroleum Monograph Series 1).

1596. Chamberlain, Neil W. , Pierson, Frank C. and
       Wolfson, Theresa, eds. A Decade of Industrial
Relations Research, 1946-1956.

1597. Cochran, Thomas C. The American Business
       System: A Historical Perspective, 1900-1955.
Cambridge: Harvard University Press, 1957.

1598. De Chazeau, Melvin G. and Kahn, Alfred E. Inte-
       gration and Competition in the Petroleum Industry.
New Haven: Yale University Press, 1959. (Petroleum
Monograph Series 3).

1599. Engler, Robert. The Politics of Oil: A Study of
       Private Power and Democratic Directions. New
York: Macmillan, 1961.

1600. Heald, Morrell. The Social Responsibilities of
       Business: Company and Community 1900-1960.
Cleveland: Press of Case Western Reserve University, 1970.

1601. Keezer, Dexter Merriam and others. New Forces
       in American Business: An Analysis of the Economic
Outlook for the '60s. New York: McGraw-Hill, 1959.

1602. Lane, Robert E. The Regulation of Businessmen: Social Conditions of Government Economic Control. Hamden, Conn., Archon Books, 1966. First published New Haven University Press, 1966. (Yale Studies in Political Science, 1).

1603. Leeman, Wayne A. The Price of Middle East Oil: An Essay in Political Economy. Ithaca: Cornell University Press, 1962.

1604. Lichtblau, John H. and Spriggs, Dillard P. The Oil Depletion Issue. New York: Petroleum Industry Research Foundation, 1959.

1605. Nash, Gerald D. United States Oil Policy, 1890-1964: Business and Government in Twentieth Century America. Pittsburgh, University of Pittsburgh Press, 1968.

1606. Rostow, Eugene V. A National Policy for the Oil Industry. New Haven: Yale University Press, 1948.

1607. Sutton, Francis X., Harris, Seymour Edwin, Kaysen, Carl and Tobin, James. The American Business Creed. Cambridge: Harvard University Press, 1956.

1608. White, Lawrence J. The Automobile Industry Since 1945. Cambridge: Harvard University Press, 1971.

1609. Whyte, William H. and the Editors of Fortune. Is Anybody Listening? How and Why U.S. Business Fumbles ... New York: Simon & Schuster, 1952.

1610. Zeigler, Harmon. The Politics of Small Business. Washington: Public Affairs Press, 1961.

6. Foreign Aid and Trade

1611. American Assembly. International Stability and Progress: United States Interests and Instruments. Background Papers. New York: American Assembly, Graduate School of Business, Columbia University, 1957.

1612. Amuzegar, Jahangir, "Point Four: Performance and Prospects," Political Science Quarterly, LXXIII (December, 1958), 530-546.

1613. Baldwin, David A. Economic Development and

American Foreign Policy, 1943-62. Chicago: University of Chicago Press, 1966.

1614.   Bauer, Raymond A. , Pool, Ithiel de Sola, and
        Dexter, Lewis A. American Business and Public
Policy: The Politics of Foreign Trade. New York: Atherton
Press, 1963.

1615.   Brodkin, E. I. , "United States Aid to India and
        Pakistan: The Attitudes of the Fifties," International
Affairs (London), XLIII (October, 1967), 664-677.

1616.   Brown, William A. and Opie, Redvers. American
        Foreign Assistance. Washington: Brookings Institution,
1953.

1617.   Castle, Eugene Winston. The Great Giveaway: The
        Realities of Foreign Aid. Chicago: Regnery, 1957.

1618.   Degler, Carl N. , "The Great Revolution in American
        Foreign Policy," Virginia Quarterly Review, XXXVIII
(Summer, 1962), 380-399.

1619.   Di Bacco, Thomas V. , "American Business and
        Foreign Aid: The Eisenhower Years," Business History Review, XLI (Spring, 1967), 21-35.

1620.   Ellis, Howard S. The Economics of Freedom: The
        Progress and Future of Aid to Europe. New York:
Published for the Council on Foreign Relations by Harper,
1950.

1621.   Espy, Willard R. Bold New Program. New York:
        Harper, 1950.

1622.   Feis, Herbert. Foreign Aid and Foreign Policy.
        New York: St. Martin Press, 1964.

1623.   Ferrell, Robert H. and Hess, Jerry N. , eds.
        Conference of Scholars on the European Recovery
Program, March 20-21, 1964. Independence, Mo. : Harry
S. Truman Library Institute for National and International
Affairs, 1964.

1624.   Gardner, Richard N. Sterling-Dollar Diplomacy:
        Anglo-American Collaboration in the Reconstruction
of Multi-Lateral Trade. Rev. ed. New York: Oxford

University Press, 1969.

1625.   Gorter, Wytze.   United States Shipping Policy.   New
         York: Published for the Council on Foreign Relations
by Harper, 1956.

1626.   Harris, Seymour Edwin.   European Recovery Program.
         Cambridge: Harvard University Press, 1948.

1627.   Hickman, Charles Addison.   Our Farm Program and
         Foreign Trade: A Conflict of National Policies.   New
York: Council on Foreign Relations, 1949.

1628.   Hitchens, Harold L. , "Influences on the Congressional
         Decision to Pass the Marshall Plan," Western Politi-
cal Quarterly, XXI (March, 1968), 51-68.

1629.   Jones, Joseph Marion.   The Fifteen Weeks:
         February 21-June 5, 1947.   New York: Viking
Press, 1955.

1630.   Kennan, George F. , "Foreign Aid in the Framework
         of National Policy," Proceedings of the Academy of
Political Science, XXIII (January, 1950), 448-458.

1631.   Krout, John A. , ed.   "The American Foreign Aid
         Program," Proceedings of the Academy of Political
Science, XXIII (January, 1950), 355-466.

1632.   Lewis, Cleona.   The United States and Foreign
         Investment Problems.   Washington: Brookings Insti-
tution, 1948.

1633.   Lewis, John Prior.   Quiet Crisis in India: Economic
         Development and American Policy.   Washington:
Brookings Institution, 1962.

1634.   Lilienthal, David E.   The Journals of David E.
         Lilienthal.   New York: Harper & Row, 1964-1971.
5 vols.   Vol. V.

1635.   Magdoff, Harry.   The Age of Imperialism: The
         Economics of U. S. Foreign Policy.   New York:
Monthly Review Press, 1969.

1636.   Mallalieu, William C. , "The Origin of the Marshall
         Plan: A Study in Policy Formation and National

Leadership," Political Science Quarterly, LXXIII (December, 1958), 481-504.

1637.   Mayer, Herbert C.   German Recovery and the Mar-
         shall Plan, 1948-1952.   New York: Edition Atlantic
Forum, 1969.

1638.   Millikan, Max F. and Rostow, Walt W.   A Proposal:
         Key to an Effective Foreign Policy.   New York:
Harper, 1957.

1639.   Montgomery, John D.   The Politics of Foreign Aid:
         American Experience in Southeast Asia.   New York:
Published for the Council on Foreign Relations by Praeger,
1962.

1640.   Nichols, Jeannette P. , "United States Aid to South
         and Southeast Asia, 1950-1960," Pacific Historical
Review, XXXII (May, 1963), 171-84.

1641.   Price, Harry Bayard.   The Marshall Plan and Its
         Meaning.   Ithaca: Cornell University Press, 1955.
Published under the auspices of the Governmental Affairs
Institute, Washington, D. C.

1642.   Quade, Quentin L. , "The Truman Administration and
         the Separation of Power: The Case of the Marshall
Plan," Review of Politics, XXVII (January, 1965), 58-77.

1643.   Randall, Clarence B.   The Communist Challenge to
         American Business.   Boston: Little, Brown, 1959.

1644.   Rippy, J. Fred, "U. S. Government Assistance to the
         Underdeveloped Countries, 1945-1953," Inter-American
Economic Affairs, VIII (Spring, 1955), 43-57.

1645.   Thorp, Willard L.   Trade, Aid, or What?   Baltimore:
         Johns Hopkins Press, 1954.

1646.   U. S. Congress.   Senate.   Committee on Foreign
         Relations.   The European Recovery Plan: Basic
Documents and Background Information.   Washington: Government Printing Office, 1947.   (80th Cong. , 1st Sess.)

1647.   Walters, Robert S.   American & Soviet Aid: A
         Comparative Analysis.   Pittsburgh, University of
Pittsburgh Press, 1970.

1648.   Ward, Barbara.   The Rich Nations and the Poor
        Nations. New York: Norton, 1962.

1649.   Westwood, Andrew F.   Foreign Aid in a Foreign
        Policy Framework. Washington: Brookings Institu-
tion, 1966.

1650.   Wiggins, James W. and Schoeck, Helmut, eds.
        Foreign Aid Reexamined: A Critical Appraisal.
Washington: Public Affairs Press, 1958.

1651.   Wolf, Charles.   Foreign Aid: Theory and Practice
        in Southern Asia. Princeton: Princeton University
Press, 1960.

1652.   Woodbridge, George, ed.   UNRRA: The History of
        the United Nations Relief and Rehabilitation Adminis-
tration. New York: Columbia University Press, 1950.
3 vols.

1653.   Young, Arthur N.   China and the Helping Hand, 1937-
        1945. Cambridge: Harvard University Press, 1963.

7. Conservation

1654.   Bartley, Ernest R.   The Tidelands Oil Controversy:
        A Legal and Historical Analysis. Austin: University
of Texas Press, 1953.

1655.   Clark, Wesley C. , "Proposed Valley Authority
        Legislation," American Political Science Review,
XL (February, 1946), 62-70.

1656.   Dodds, Gordon B.   "The Historiography of American
        Conservation: Past and Prospects," Pacific Northwest
Quarterly, LVI (April, 1965), 75-81.

1657.   Golzé, Alfred R.   Reclamation in the United States.
        Caldwell, Ida. , Caxton Printers, 1961.

1658.   Hart, Henry C.   The Dark Missouri.   Madison:
        University of Wisconsin Press, 1957.

1659.   _____. , "Valley Development and Valley Adminis-
        tration in the Missouri Basin," Public Administration
Review, VIII (Winter, 1948), 1-11.

1660.   Leuchtenburg, William E.   Flood Control Politics:
        The Connecticut River Valley Problem, 1927-1950.
Cambridge: Harvard University Press, 1953.

1661.   Raushenbush, Stephen, ed.   "The Future of Our
        Natural Resources," American Academy of Political
and Social Science.   Annals, CCLXXXI (May, 1952), 1-202.

1662.   Ridgeway, Marian E.   The Missouri Basin's Pick-
        Sloan: A Case Study in Congressional Determination.
Urbana: University of Illinois Press, 1955.   (Illinois Studies
in the Social Sciences, Vol. 35).

1663.   "A Symposium on Regional Planning," Iowa Law
        Review, XXXII (January, 1947), 193-406.

8. Labor

    a.   General

1664.   Aaron, Benjamin, "Amending the Taft-Hartley Act:
        A Decade of Frustration," Industrial and Labor Rela-
tions Review, XI (April, 1958), 327-338.

1665.   American Enterprise Association.   Labor Unions and
        Public Policy, by Edward H. Chamberlin and others.
Washington: American Enterprise Association, 1958.

1666.   Boarman, Patrick M.   Union Monopolies and Anti-
        Trust Restraints.   Washington: Labor Policy Associa-
tion, 1963.

1667.   Bradley, Philip D. , ed.   The Public Stake in Union
        Power.   Charlottesville: The University of Virginia
Press, 1959.

1668.   Ching, Cyrus S.   Review and Reflection: A Half-
        Century of Labor Relations.   New York: B. C.
Forbes and Sons, 1953.

1669.   Claque, Ewan, "Interrelationship of Prices, Wages,
        and Productivity, 1946-57," U.S. Monthly Labor
Review, LXXXI (January, 1958), 14-22.

1670.   Cole, Gordon H. , Stein, Leon, and Sobol, Norman,
        eds.   Labor's Story As Reported by the American
Labor Press.   Glen Cove, N.Y. , Community Publishers,
1961.

1671.   Einzig, Paul.   The Economic Consequences of Auto-
        mation.   New York: Norton, 1957.

1672.   Gabarino, Joseph William.   Wage Policy and Long-
        Term Contracts.   Washington: Brookings Institution,
1962.

1673.   Goldberg, Joseph P. , "Labor - Management Since
        World War II," Current History, XLVIII, 346-352
(June, 1965), 365-366.

1674.   Gregory, Charles O.   Labor and the Law.   2nd rev.
        ed with 1961 Supplement.   New York: Norton, 1961.
First published 1946.

1675.   Harbison, Frederick H. , and Spencer, Robert C. ,
        "The Politics of Collective Bargaining: The Postwar
Record in Steel," American Political Science Review, XLVIII
(September, 1954), 705-720.

1676.   Hawley, Ellis W. , "The Politics of the Mexican
        Labor Issue, 1950-1955," Agricultural History, XL
(July, 1966), 157-176.

1677.   Kaplan, Abraham D. H. , The Guarantee of Annual
        Wages.   Washington: Brookings Institution, 1947.

1678.   Lens, Sidney.   Left, Right & Center: Conflicting
        Forces in American Labor.   Hinsdale, Ill. , Regnery,
1949.

1679.   McClure, Arthur F.   The Truman Administration and
        the Problems of Post-War Labor, 1945-1948.   Ruther-
ford, N. J. :   Fairleigh Dickinson University Press, [1969].

1680.   Millis, Harry A. and Brown, Emily Clark.   From
        the Wagner Act to Taft-Hartley: A Study of National
Labor Policy and Labor Relations.   Chicago: University of
Chicago Press, 1950.

1681.   Mills, Charles Wright.   The New Men of Power:
        America's Labor Leaders.   New York: Harcourt,
Brace, 1948.

1682.   Peterson, Florence.   Survey of Labor Economics.
        Rev. ed.   New York: Harper, 1951.

1683.   Radosh, Ronald.   American Labor and United States
        Foreign Policy.   New York: Random House, 1969.

1684.   Rayback, Joseph G.   A History of American Labor.
        New York: Macmillan, 1959.

1685.   Scher, Seymour, "Regulatory Agency Control through
        Appointment.   The Case of the Eisenhower Adminis-
tration and the NLRB," Journal of Politics, XXIII (November,
1961), 667-688.

1686.   Seidman, Joel Isaac.   American Labor: From De-
        fense to Reconversion.   Chicago: University of
Chicago Press, 1953.

1687.   Shister, Joseph, Aaron, Benjamin, and Summers,
        Clyde W. eds.   Public Policy and Collective Bargain-
ing. New York: Harper & Row, 1962.

1688.   Somers, Gerald G. , Cushman, Edward L. and Wein-
        berg, Nat, eds.   Adjusting to Technological Change.
New York: Harper & Row, 1963.   (Industrial Relations Research Association Publication No. 29).

1689.   Taft, Philip.   Organized Labor in American History.
        New York: Harper & Row, 1964.

1690.   Walker, Charles R. and Guest, Robert H.   Man on
        the Assembly Line.   Cambridge: Harvard University
Press, 1952.

1691.   _____. Steeltown: An Industrial Case History of
        the Conflict between Progress and Security. New
York: Harper, 1950.

1692.   Warne, Colston E. and others, eds.   Labor in
        Postwar America.   Brooklyn, Remsen Press, 1949.

1693.   Woytinsky, Wladimir S. and others.   Employment
        and Wages in the United States. New York:
Twentieth Century Fund, 1953.

        b.   Labor Unions

1694.   Bernstein, Irving, "The Growth of American Unions,
        1945-1960," Labor History, II (Spring, 1961), 131-
157.

1695.   Calkins, Fay.   The CIO and the Democratic Party.
        Chicago: University of Chicago Press, 1952.

1696.   Goldberg, Arthur J.   AFL-CIO: Labor United.   New
        York: McGraw-Hill, 1956.

1697.   Hardman, Jacob B. S. and Neufeld, Maurice F. , eds.
        The House of Labor: Internal Operations of American
Unions.   New York: Prentice-Hall, 1951.

1698.   Herling, John.   Right to Challenge: People and Power
        in the Steelworkers Union.   New York: Harper &
Row, 1971.

1699.   Howe, Irving and Widick, B. J.   The U. A. W. and
        Walter Reuther.   New York: Random House, 1949.

1700.   Hutchinson, John.   The Imperfect Union: A History
        of Corruption in American Trade Unions.   New York:
Dutton, 1970.

1701.   James, Ralph C. and James, Estelle Dinerstein.
        Hoffa and the Teamsters: A Study of Union Power.
Princeton: Van Nostrand, 1965.

1702.   Kampelman, Max M.   The Communist Party vs. the
        C. I. O. : A Study in Power Politics.   New York:
Praeger, 1957.

1703.   Kennedy, Robert F.   The Enemy Within.   New York:
        Harper, 1960.

1704.   Krislov, Joseph, "Organizing Union Growth, and the
        Cycle, 1949-1966," Labor History, XI (Spring, 1970),
212-222.

1705.   Lens, Sidney.   The Crisis of American Labor.   New
        York: Sagamore Press, 1959.

1706.   Lieberman, Elias.   Unions before the War: Historic
        Trials Showing the Evolution of Labor Rights in the
United States.   Rev. ed.   New York: Oxford Book Co. ,
1960.

1707.   Metz, Harold W. and Jacobstein, Meyer.   A National
        Labor Policy.   Washington: Brookings Institution,
1947.

1708.   Mollenhoff, Clark R.   Tentacles of Power: The Story
        of Jimmy Hoffa.   Cleveland: World, 1965.

1709.   Saposs, David J.   Communism in American Unions.
        New York: McGraw-Hill, 1959.

1710.   Taft, Philip.   The A. F. of L. from the Death of
        Gompers to the Merger.   New York: Harper & Row,
1959.

1711.   _____.   Structure and Government of Labor Unions.
        Cambridge: Harvard University Press, 1954.

1712.   Velie, Lester.   Labor U. S. A.   New York: Harper,
        1959.

1713.   Wolfe, Arthur C., "Trends in Labor Union Voting
        Behavior, 1948-1968," Industrial Relations, IX
(October, 1969), 1-10.

1714.   Wright, David McCord, ed.   The Impact of the
        Union: Eight Economic Theorists Evaluate the Labor
Union Movement.   New York: Harcourt, Brace, 1951.

        c.   Labor Legislation

1715.   Bell, Daniel, "Taft-Hartley, Five Years Old,"
        Fortune, XLVI (July, 1952), 69, 172.

1716.   Brown, Emily Clark.   National Labor Policy: Taft-
        Hartley after Three Years and the Next Steps.
Washington: Public Affairs Institute, 1950.   (Public Affairs
Institute, Washington, D. C.   Report No. 6).

1717.   Colm, Gerhard, ed.   The Employment Act: Past and
        Future: A Tenth Anniversary Symposium.   Washington:
National Planning Association, 1956.   (Special Report No. 41).

1718.   Flash, Edward S.   Economic Advice and Presidential
        Leadership: The Council of Economic Advisers.   New
York: Columbia University Press, 1965.

1719.   Hartley, Fred Allan.   Our New National Labor Policy:
        The Taft Hartley Act and the Next Steps.   New York:
Funk & Wagnalls, 1948.

1720.   Kesselman, Louis Coleridge.   The Social Politics

of FEPC: A Study in Reform Pressure Movements.
Chapel Hill: University of North Carolina Press, 1948.

1721. Lee, R. Alton. Truman and Taft-Hartley: A Question
       of Mandate. Lexington: University of Kentucky Press,
1966.

1722. Leek, John H. Government and Labor in the United
       States. New York: Rinehart, 1952.

1723. Luck, Thomas J. , "Effects of the Taft-Hartley Act
       on Labor Agreements, 1947-1952," Southern Economic
Journal, XX (October, 1953), 145-155.

1724. McAdams, Alan K. Power and Politics in Labor
       Legislation. New York: Columbia University Press,
1964.

1725. Maslow, Will, "FEPC--A Case History in Parliamen-
       tary Maneuver," University of Chicago Law Review,
XIII (June, 1946), 407-444.

1726. Nourse, Edwin G. Economics in the Public Service:
       Administrative Aspects of the Employment Act. New
York: Harcourt, Brace, 1953.

1727. Pomper, Gerald, "Labor and Congress: The Repeal of
       Taft-Hartley," Labor History, II (Fall, 1961), 323-343.

1728. _____, "Labor Legislation: The Revision of Taft-
       Hartley in 1953-1954," Labor History, VI (Spring,
       1965), 143-158.

1729. Reilly, Gerard D. , "The Legislative History of the
       Taft-Hartley Act," George Washington Law Review,
XXIX (December, 1960), 285-300.

1730. Ruchames, Louis. Race, Jobs and Politics: The
       Story of FEPC. New York: Columbia University
Press, 1953.

1731. Seligman, Lester G. , "Presidential Leadership: The
       Inner Circle and Institutionalization," Journal of
Politics, XVIII (August, 1956), 416 ff.

1732. Slichter, Sumner Huber, "Revision of the Taft-Hartley
       Act. " Quarterly Journal of Economics, LXVII

(May, 1953), 149-180.

1733. _____. "The Taft-Hartley Act," Quarterly Journal of Economics, LXIII (February, 1949), 1-31.

1734. "The Taft-Hartley Act after Ten Years, A Symposium," Industrial and Labor Relations Review, XI (April, 1958), 327-412.

1735. U.S. National Labor Relations Board. Legislative History of the Labor-Management Reporting and Disclosure Act of 1959. Washington: Government Printing Office, 1959. 2 vols.

   d.   Labor Disputes

1736. Bernstein, Barton J., "The Truman Administration and Its Reconversion Wage Policy," Labor History, VI (Fall, 1965), 214-231.

1737. _____., "The Truman Administration and the Steel Strike of 1946," Journal of American History, LII (March, 1966), 791-803.

1738. _____., "Walter Reuther and the General Motors Strike of 1945-46," Michigan History, XLIX (September, 1965), 260-277.

1739. Bernstein, Irving, Enarson, Harold L., and Fleming, R. W., eds. Emergency Disputes and National Policy. New York: Harper, 1966. (Industrial Relations Research Association Publication 15).

1740. Blackman, John L. Presidential Seizure in Labor Disputes. Cambridge: Harvard University Press, 1967.

1741. Chamberlain, Neil W. and Schilling, Jane Metzger. The Impact of Strikes: Their Social and Economic Costs. New York: Harper, 1954.

1742. _____. Social Responsibility and Strikes. New York: Harper, 1953.

1743. Hoch, Myron, "The Oil Strike of 1945," Southern Economic Journal, XV (October, 1948), 117-133.

1744.   Karsh, Bernard.   Diary of a Strike.   Urbana:
         University of Illinois Press, 1958.

1745.   Rees, Albert E. , "The Economic Impact of Collective
         Bargaining in the Steel and Coal Industries During the
Post-War Period," Industrial Relations Research Association
Proceedings, III (December, 1950), 203-212.

1746.   Taylor, George W.   Government Regulation of Indus-
         trial Relations.   New York: Prentice-Hall, 1948.

1747.   Westin, Alan F. , ed.   The Anatomy of a Constitu-
         tional Law Case: Youngstown Sheet and Tube Co.
v. Sawyer; The Steel Seizure Decision.   New York:
Macmillan, 1958.

     e.   Labor Supply

1748.   Haber, William and others.   Manpower in the United
         States: Problems and Policies.   N. Y. : Harper, 1954.

1749.   Jaffe, Abram J. and Stewart, Charles D.   Manpower
         Resources and Utilization: Principles of Working
Force Analysis.   New York: Wiley, 1951.

1750.   Morton, Walter A. , "Trade Unionism, Full Employ-
         ment and Inflation," American Economic Review, XL
(March, 1950), 13-39.

1751.   Rees, Albert E. , "Postwar Wage Determination in the
         Basic Steel Industry," American Economic Review,
XLI (June, 1951), 389-404.

1752.   _____. , "Wage-Price Relations in the Basic Steel
         Industry, 1945-1948," Industrial and Labor Relations
Review, VI (January, 1953), 195-205.

1753.   Stein, Bruno, "Wage Stabilization in the Korean War
         Period: The Role of the Subsidiary Wage Boards,"
Labor History, IV (Spring, 1963), 161-177.

VI.   SOCIAL AND INTELLECTUAL TRENDS

A.   COMMUNICATION

1.   The Printed Page

1754.   Berelson, Bernard.   The Library's Public.   New
York: Columbia University Press, 1949.   (A Report
of the Public Library Inquiry).

1755.   Leigh, Robert D.   The Public Library in the United
States: The General Report of the Public Library
Inquiry of the Social Science Research Council.   New York:
Columbia University Press, 1950.

1756.   Miller, William.   The Book Industry: A Report of the
Public Library Inquiry.   New York: Columbia University Press, 1949.

1757.   Talese, Gay.   The Kingdom and the Power.   New
York: World, 1969.   History of the New York Times
in recent years.

2.   Advertising

1758.   McLuhan, Herbert Marshall.   The Mechanical Bride:
Folklore of Industrial Man.   New York: Vanguard
Press, 1951.

1759.   Mayer, Martin.   Madison Avenue, U.S.A.   New York:
Harper, 1958.

3.   The Mass Media

1760.   Barnouw, Erik.   A History of Broadcasting in the
United States.   New York: Oxford University Press,
1966-1970.   3 vols.   Vols. II and III.

1761.   Bogart, Leo.   The Age of Television: A Study of
Viewing Habits and the Impact of Television on
American Life.   2d ed. rev. and enl.   New York: Ungar,

1958. First published 1956.

1762. Columbia University. Bureau of Applied Social Re-
       search. People Look at Radio. Chapel Hill: Uni-
versity of North Carolina Press, 1946. A study directed by
Paul F. Lazarsfeld. Report on a survey conducted by the
National Opinion Research Center, University of Denver,
Harry Field Director, Analyzed and interpreted by the Bureau
of Applied Social Research, Columbia University.

1763. Commission on Freedom of the Press. The American
       Radio by Llewellyn White. Chicago: University of
Chicago Press, 1947.

1764. _____. A Free and Responsible Press: A General
       Report on Mass Communication ... Chicago: Univer-
sity of Chicago Press, 1947.

1765. Elliott, William Yandell, ed. Television's Impact on
       American Culture. East Lansing, Michigan State
University Press, 1956.

1766. Inglis, R. A. Freedom of the Movies: A Report on
       Self Regulation from the Commission on Freedom of
the Press. Chicago: University of Chicago Press, 1947.

1767. Klapper, Joseph T. The Effects of Mass Communi-
       cation. Glencoe, Ill. : Free Press, 1960.

1768. Powdermaker, Hortense. Hollywood, the Dream
       Factory: An Anthropologist Looks at the Movie-
Makers. Boston: Little Brown, 1950.

1769. Rosenberg, Bernard and White, David M. , eds.
       Mass Culture: The Popular Arts in America.
Glencoe, Ill. : Free Press, 1957.

1770. Schramm, Wilbur L. , Lyle, Jack, and Parker,
       Edwin B. Television in the Lives of Our Children.
Stanford: Stanford University Press, 1961.

1771. Seldes, Gilbert. The Great Audience. New York:
       Viking Press, 1950.

1772. _____. The Public Arts. New York: Simon &
       Schuster, 1956.

1773. Siepmann, Charles A. Radio, Television and Society.
       New York: Oxford University Press, 1950.

1774. Thomson, Charles A. H. Television and Presidential
       Politics: The Experience in 1952 and the Problems
Ahead. Washington: Brookings Institution, 1956.

1775. Wolfenstein, Martha and Leites, Nathan. Movies: A
       Psychological Study. Glencoe, Ill. : Free Press,
1950.

                    B.   SCHOOLS OF THOUGHT

1776. Auerbach, M. Morton. The Conservative Illusion.
       New York: Columbia University Press, 1959.

1777. Bell, Daniel, ed. The New American Right. New
       York: Criterion Books, 1955.

1778. _____, ed. The Radical Right: The New American
       Right Expanded and Updated. Garden City: Doubleday,
1963.

1779. Buckley, William F. Up from Liberalism. New
       York: McDowell, Obolensky, 1959.

1780. The Conservative Papers, with an introduction by
       Melvin Laird. Chicago: Quadrangle Books, 1964.

1781. Ekirch, Arthur A. The Decline of American Liber-
       alism. New York: Longmans, Green, 1955.

1782. Girvetz, Harry K. From Wealth to Welfare: The
       Evolution of Liberalism. Stanford: Stanford Univer-
sity Press, 1950.

1783. Kendall, Willmoore. The Conservative Affirmation.
       Chicago: Regnery, 1963.

1784. Kirk, Russell. A Program for Conservatives.
       Chicago: Regnery, 1954.

1785. McCarthy, Eugene J. A Liberal Answer to the Con-
       servative Challenge. New York: Praeger, 1965.

1786. Meyer, Frank S. , ed. What is Conservatism?

New York: Holt, Rinehart and Winston, 1964.

1787.   Newman, William J.   The Futilitarian Society.
        New York: Braziller, 1961.

1788.   Pennock, James Roland.   Liberal Democracy: Its
        Merits and Prospects.   New York: Rinehart, 1950.

1789.   Perkins, Dexter.   The American Way.   Ithaca:
        Cornell University Press, 1957.

1790.   Roosevelt, James, ed.   The Liberal Papers.
        Chicago: Quadrangle Books, 1962.

1791.   Rossiter, Clinton.   Conservatism in America: The
        Thankless Persuasion.   2d ed.   New York: Knopf,
1962.   First published 1955.

1792.   Schlesinger, Arthur M.   The Vital Center: The
        Politics of Freedom.   Boston: Houghton Mifflin,
1962.

1793.   Wilson, Francis.   The Case for Conservatism: Three
        Lectures Delivered at the University of Washington.
Seattle: Universtiy of Washington Press, 1951.

C.   EDUCATION

1794.   Barzun, Jacques.   The House of Intellect.   New
        York: Harper, 1959.

1795.   _____.   Teacher in America.   Boston: Little,
        Brown, 1945.

1796.   Benton, William.   This Is the Challenge: The Benton
        Reports of 1956-1958 on the Nature of the Soviet
Threat.   New York: Associated Colleges Press, 1958.

1797.   Bestor, Arthur E.   Educational Wastelands: The
        Retreat from Learning in Our Public Schools.
Urbana: University of Illinois Press, 1953.

1798.   _____.   The Restoration of American Learning:
        A Program for Redeeming the Unfulfilled Promise of
American Education.   New York: Knopf, 1955.

1799. Brameld, Theodore. Toward a Reconstructed Philosophy of Education. New York: Dryden Press, 1956.

1800. Conant, James B. The American High School Today: A First Report to Interested Citizens. New York: McGraw-Hill, 1959.

1801. _____. The Child, the Parent, and the State. Cambridge: Harvard University Press, 1959.

1802. _____. The Citadel of Learning. New Haven: Yale University Press, 1956.

1803. _____. Education in a Divided World: The Function of the Public Schools in Our Unique Society. Cambridge: Harvard University Press, 1948.

1804. _____. Slums and Suburbs: A Commentary on Schools in Metropolitan Areas. New York: McGraw-Hill, 1961.

1805. Fine, Benjamin. Our Children Are Cheated: The Crisis in American Education. New York: Holt, 1947.

1806. Fletcher, Cyril Scott, ed. Education for Public Responsibility. New York: Norton, 1961.

1807. Ginzberg, Eli and Bray, Douglas W. The Uneducated. New York: Columbia University Press, 1953.

1808. Havemann, Ernest and West, Patricia S. They Went to College: The College Graduate in America Today. New York: Harcourt, Brace, 1952.

1809. Hechinger, Fred M. An Adventure in Education: Connecticut Points the Way. New York: Macmillan, 1956.

1810. Hulburd, David. This Happened in Pasadena. New York: Macmillan, 1951.

1811. Jones, Howard Mumford. One Great Society: Humane Learning in the United States. New York: Harcourt, Brace, 1959.

1812. Melby, Ernest O. American Education under Fire:

The Story of the "Phony Three-R Fight." New York:
Anti-Defamation League of B'nai B'rith, 1951.

1813.   Rickover, Hyman G.   Education and Freedom.   New
        York: Dutton, 1959.

1814.   Riesman, David.   Constraint and Variety in American
        Education.   Lincoln: University of Nebraska Press,
1956.

1815.   Ulich, Robert.   Crisis and Hope in American Educa-
        tion. Boston: Beacon Press, 1951.

1816.   U.S. President's Commission on Higher Education.
        Higher Education for American Democracy.   Washing-
ton: Government Printing Office, 1947.   6 vols.

1817.   Woodring, Paul A.   A Fourth of a Nation.   New
        York: McGraw-Hill, 1957.

                D.   THE SCIENTISTS' ROLE

1818.   Burrow, James G.   AMA: Voice of American Medi-
        cine. Baltimore: Johns Hopkins Press, 1963.

1819.   Bush, Vannevar.   Modern Arms and Free Men: A
        Discussion of the Role of Science in Preserving
Democracy.   New York: Simon & Schuster, 1949.

1820.   Conant, James B.   Modern Science and Modern Man.
        New York: Columbia University Press, 1952.

1821.   Dupre, Joseph Stefan and Lakoff, Sanford A.   Science
        and the Nation: Policy and Politics.   Englewood
Cliffs, N.J. , Prentice-Hall, 1962.

1822.   Gilpin, Robert.   American Scientists and Nuclear
        Weapons Policy.   Princeton: Princeton University
Press, 1962.

1823.   _____. and Wright, Christopher, eds.   Scientists
        and National Policy-Making.   New York: Columbia
University Press, 1964.

1824.   Greenberg, Daniel S.   The Politics of Pure Science.
        New York: New American Library, 1967.

1825.   Lasby, Clarence G.   Project Paperclip: German
        Scientists and the Cold War.   New York: Atheneum,
1971.

1826.   Nieburg, Harold L.   In the Name of Science.
        Chicago: Quadrangle Books, 1966.

1827.   Oppenheimer, J. Robert.   The Open Mind.   New
        York: Simon & Schuster, 1955.

1828.   Price, Don Krasher.   Government and Science: Their
        Dynamic Relation in American Democracy.   New
York: New York University Press, 1954.

1829.   Rabinowitch, Eugene.   The Dawn of a New Age:
        Reflections on Science and Human Affairs.   Chicago:
University of Chicago Press, 1963.

1830.   Sherwood, Morgan, "Federal Policy for Basic
        Research: Presidential Staff and the National Science
Foundation, 1950-1956," Journal of American History, LV
(December, 1968), 599-615.

1831.   Skolnikoff, Eugene B.   Science, Technology, and
        American Foreign Policy.   Cambridge: M. I. T. Press,
1967.

1832.   Smith, Alice Kimball.   A Peril and a Hope: The
        Scientists' Movement in America, 1945-1957.
Chicago: University of Chicago Press, 1965.

1833.   Strickland, Donald A.   Scientists in Politics: The
        Atomic Scientists' Movement, 1945-46.   Lafayette,
Ind. :   Purdue University Studies, 1968.

1834.   U. S. President's Scientific Research Board.   Science
        and Public Policy: A Report to the President by John
R. Steelman.   Washington: Government Printing Office,
1947.   5 vols.

E.   RELIGION IN AMERICA

1835.   Blanshard, Paul.   American Freedom and Catholic
        Power.   2d ed. rev. and enl.   Boston: Beacon
Press, 1958.

1836. Cogley, John, ed. Religion in America: Original Essays on Religion in a Free Society. New York: Meridian Books, 1958.

1837. Dawson, Joseph Martin. America's Way in Church, State, and Society. New York: Macmillan, 1953.

1838. Herberg, Will. Protestant, Catholic, Jew: An Essay in American Religious Sociology. Rev. ed. Garden City: Doubleday, 1960.

1839. Jorstad, Erling. The Politics of Doomsday: Fundamentalists of the Far Right. Nashville, Tenn.: Abingdon Press, 1970.

1840. Kane, John J. Catholic-Protestant Conflicts in America. Chicago: Regnery, 1955.

1841. Lincoln, Charles Eric. The Black Muslims in America. Boston: Beacon Press, 1961.

1842. O'Dea, Thomas F. American Catholic Dilemma: An Inquiry into the Intellectual Life. New York: Sheed and Ward, 1958.

1843. O'Neill, James Milton. Catholicism and American Freedom. New York: Harper, 1952.

1844. Pfeffer, Leo. Creeds in Competition: A Creative Force in American Culture. New York: Harper, 1958.

1845. Shields, Currin V. Democracy and Catholicism in America. New York: McGraw-Hill, 1958.

F. SOCIAL CONDITIONS

1. General

1846. Anderson, Martin. The Federal Bulldozer: A Critical Analysis of Urban Renewal, 1949-1962. Cambridge: Massachusetts Institute of Technology Press, 1964.

1847. Bates, Marston. The Prevalence of People. New York: Scribner, 1955.

1848. Bell, Daniel. The End of Ideology: On the Exhaustion
       of Political Ideas in the Fifties. Glencoe, Ill.: Free
Press, 1960.

1849. Bendix, Reinhard and Lipset, Seymour M. eds.
       Class, Status and Power: Social Stratification in
Comparative Perspective. 2d ed. New York: Free Press,
1966. First published 1953.

1850. Bogue, Donald J. The Population of the United
       States. Glencoe, Ill.: Free Press, 1959.

1851. Brooks, John N. The Great Leap: The Past Twenty-
       five Years in America. New York: Harper & Row,
1966.

1852. Brown, Harrison. The Challenge of Man's Future:
       An Inquiry Concerning the Condition of Man During
the Years That Lie Ahead. New York: Viking Press, 1954.

1853. Centers, Richard. The Psychology of Social Classes:
       A Study of Class Consciousness. New York: Russell
and Russell, 1949.

1854. Clark, Thomas D. The Emerging South. New York:
       Oxford University Press, 1961.

1855. Davis, Joseph S., "Our Changed Population Outlook,"
       American Economic Review, XLII (June, 1952), 304-
325.

1856. De Grazia, Sebastian. Of Time, Work and Leisure.
       New York: Twentieth Century Fund, 1962.

1857. Divine, Robert A. American Immigration Policy,
       1924-1952. New Haven: Yale University Press, 1957.

1858. Domhoff, G. William and Ballard, Hoyt B., comps.
       C. Wright Mills and the Power Elite. Boston:
Beacon Press, 1968.

1859. Donaldson, Scott. The Suburban Myth. New York:
       Columbia University Press, 1969.

1860. Hauser, Philip Morris. Population Perspectives.
       New Brunswick, N.J.: Rutgers University Press,
1961.

1861. Hollingshead, August. Elmtown's Youth: The Impact of
       Social Classes on Adolescents. New York: Wiley,
1949.

1862. Jacobs, Jane. The Death and Life of Great American
       Cities. New York: Random House, 1961.

1863. Kariel, Henry S. The Decline of American Pluralism.
       Stanford: Stanford University Press, 1961.

1864. Kempton, Murray. America Comes of Middle Age:
       Columns, 1950-1962. Boston: Little, Brown, 1963.

1865. Kornhauser, Arthur W. ed. Problems of Power in
       American Democracy. Detroit: Wayne State Univer-
sity Press, 1957.

1866. Lantz, Herman R. and McCrary, J. C. People of
       Coal Town. New York: Columbia University Press,
1958.

1867. Lipset, Seymour M. and Lowenthal, Leo, eds. Cul-
       ture and Social Character: The Work of David Riesman
Reviewed. Glencoe, Ill. : Free Press, 1961.

1868. McWilliams, Carey. A Mask for Privilege: Anti-
       Semitism in America. Boston: Little, Brown, 1948.

1869. Martin, Ralph G. The Best Is None Too Good. New
       York: Farrar, Straus, 1948.

1870. Mills, Charles Wright. The Power Elite. New
       York: Oxford University Press, 1956.

1871. _____. The Sociological Imagination. New York:
       Oxford University Press, 1959.

1872. _____. White Collar: The American Middle
       Classes. New York: Oxford University Press, 1951.

1873. Monsen, R. Joseph and Cannon, Mark W. The
       Makers of Public Policy: American Power Groups
and Their Ideologies. New York: McGraw-Hill, 1965.

1874. Mumford, Lewis. The City in History: Its Origins,
       Its Transformations, and Its Prospects. New York:
Harcourt, Brace & World, 1961.

1875.   Neustadt, Richard E., "Congress and the Fair Deal:
        A Legislative Balance Sheet," Public Policy, V
        (1954), 349-381.

1876.   Packard, Vance. The Hidden Persuaders. New
        York: McKay, 1957.

1877.   _____. The Status Seekers: An Exploration of
        Class Behavior in America and the Hidden Barriers
        That Affect You ... New York: McKay, 1959.

1878.   Petersen, William. The Politics of Population.
        Garden City: Doubleday, 1964.

1879.   Potter, David M. People of Plenty: Economic
        Abundance and the American Character. Chicago:
        University of Chicago Press, 1954.

1880.   Rainwater, Lee, Coleman, Richard P. and Handel,
        Gerald. Workingman's Wife: Her Personality, World
        and Life Style. New York: Oceana Publications, 1959.

1881.   Reissman, Leonard. Class in American Society.
        Glencoe, Ill.: Free Press, 1960.

1882.   Riesman, David and Glazer, Nathan. Faces in the
        Crowd: Individual Studies in Character and Politics.
        New Haven: Yale University Press, 1952.

1883.   _____, Denney, Reuel, and Glazer, Nathan. The
        Lonely Crowd: A Study of the Changing American
        Character. New Haven: Yale University Press, 1950.

1884.   Rose, Arnold M. and Rose, Caroline. America
        Divided: Minority Group Relations in the United States.
        New York: Knopf, 1948.

1885.   Rubin, Morton. Plantation County. Chapel Hill:
        University of North Carolina Press, 1951.

1886.   Russell, James Earl, ed. National Policies for
        Education, Health and Social Services. Garden City:
        Doubleday, 1955.

1887.   Shimm, Melvin G. and Everett, Robinson O., eds.
        Population Control, the Imminent World Crisis.
        New York: Oceana Publications, 1961.

1888.   Sundquist, James L.   Politics and Policy: The Eisen-
        hower, Kennedy, and Johnson Years.   Washington:
Brookings Institution, 1968.

1889.   Warner, William Lloyd.   American Life: Dream and
        Reality.   Rev. ed.   Chicago: University of Chicago
Press, 1962.

1890.   _____, and others.   Democracy in Jonesville:
        A Study in Quality and Inequality.   New York:
Harper, 1949.

1891.   _____, Meeker, Marchia, and Eells, Kenneth.
        Social Class in America: A Manual of Procedure for
the Measurement of Social Status.   Chicago: Science Research
Associates, 1949.

1892.   Whyte, William H.   The Organization Man.   New
        York: Simon & Schuster, 1956.

1893.   Wood, Robert C.   Suburbia: Its People and Their
        Politics.   Boston: Houghton Mifflin, 1959.

2.   Crime and Delinquency

1894.   Deutsch, Albert.   Our Rejected Children.   Boston:
        Little, Brown, 1950.

1895.   Glueck, Sheldon and Glueck, Eleanor.   Unraveling
        Juvenile Delinquency.   New York: Commonwealth
Fund, 1950.

1896.   Kefauver, Estes.   Crime in America.   Edited ana
        with an introduction by Sidney Shalett.   Garden City:
Doubleday, 1951.

1897.   Scudder, Kenyon J.   Prisoners Are People.   Garden
        City: Doubleday, 1952.

3.   Woman's Role

1898.   Clover, Vernon T.   Changes in Differences in
        Earnings and Occupational Status of Men and Women,
1947-1967.   Lubbock: Department of Economics, Texas
Technical University, 1970.

1899.   Fisch, Edith L. and Schwartz, Mortimer D. , eds.

State Laws on the Employment of Women. Washington: Scarecrow Press, 1953.

1900.   Gruenberg, Sidonie M. and Krech, Hilda Sidney.
The Many Lives of Modern Woman: A Guide to
Happiness in Her Complex Role. Garden City: Doubleday,
1952.

1901.   Lundberg, Ferdinand and Farnham, Marynia F.
Modern Woman: The Lost Sex. New York: Harper,
1947.

1902.   Smuts, Robert W. Women and Work in America.
New York: Columbia University Press, 1959.

G.   AMERICAN CIVILIZATION

1903.   Allen, Frederick L. The Big Change: America
Transforms Itself, 1900-1950. New York: Harper,
1952.

1904.   Barzun, Jacques. God's Country and Mine: A
Declaration of Love Spiced with a Few Harsh Words.
Boston: Little, Brown, 1954.

1905.   Bell, Bernard Iddings. Crowd Culture: An Examination of the American Way of Life. New York:
Harper, 1952.

1906.   Boorstin, Daniel J. The Image: or, What Happened
to the American Dream. New York: Atheneum, 1962.

1907.   Chase, Richard. The Democratic Vista. Garden
City: Doubleday, 1958.

1908.   Conference on Science, Philosophy and Religion in
Their Relation to the Democratic Way of Life, Conflicts of Power in Modern Culture, ed. by Lyman Bryson,
Louis Finkelstein and R. M. MacIver. New York: Harper,
1947. (Its Symposium No. 7)

1909.   Curti, Merle. The Growth of American Thought.
3d ed. New York: Harper & Row, 1964.

1910.   Fiedler, Leslie A. An End to Innocence: Essays on
Culture and Politics. Boston: Beacon Press, 1955.

1911. Frankel, Charles. The Case for Modern Man. New York: Harper, 1956.

1912. Gardner, John W. Excellence: Can We Be Equal and Excellent Too? New York: Harper, 1961.

1913. Gold, Herbert. The Age of Happy Problems. New York: Dial Press, 1962.

1914. Goldman, Eric F., "Good-By to the 'Fifties--and Good Riddance," Harper's Magazine, CCXX (January, 1960), 27-29.

1915. Gunther, John. Inside U.S.A. Rev. ed. New York: Harper, 1951.

1916. Gurko, Leo. Heroes, Highbrows and the Popular Mind. Indianapolis: Bobbs-Merrill, 1953.

1917. Hallowell, John H. The Moral Foundations of Democracy. Chicago: University of Chicago Press, 1954.

1918. Kornhauser, William. The Politics of Mass Society. New York: Free Press, 1959.

1919. Krutch, Joseph Wood and others. Is the Common Man Too Common? Norman: University of Oklahoma Press, 1954.

1920. _____. The Measure of Man: On Freedom, Human Values, Survival and the Modern Temper. Indianapolis: Bobbs-Merrill, 1954.

1921. Lerner, Max. America As a Civilization: Life and Thought in the United States Today. New York: Simon & Schuster, 1957.

1922. Lippmann, Walter. Essays in the Public Philosophy. Boston: Little, Brown, 1955.

1923. Mumford, Lewis. In the Name of Sanity. New York: Harcourt, Brace, 1954.

1924. Niebuhr, Reinhold. Pious and Secular America. New York: Scribner, 1958.

1925.   Partisan Review. America and the Intellectuals: A
        Symposium. New York: Partisan Review, 1953.

1926.   Riesman, David. Individualism Reconsidered and
        Other Essays. Glencoe, Ill. : Free Press, 1954.

1927.   Rovere, Richard. The American Establishment and
        Other Reports, Opinions and Speculations. New York:
Harcourt, Brace & World, 1962.

1928.   Soule, George. Time for Living. New York:
        Viking Press, 1955.

1929.   Stone, Isidor F. The Haunted Fifties. New York:
        Random House, 1963.

1930.   Swados, Harvey. A Radical's America. Boston:
        Little, Brown, 1962.

1931.   Viereck, Peter. The Shame and Glory of the Intel-
        lectuals: Babbitt, Jr. vs. the Rediscovery of Values.
Boston: Beacon Press, 1953.

1932.   Wecter, Dixon and others. Changing Patterns in
        American Civilization. Philadelphia: University of
Pennsylvania Press, 1949.

Aaron, Benjamin, 1664, 1687
Abbott, Charles C. , 1568
Abbott, Roger S. , 1168
Abels, Jules, 178, 235, 1513
Abraham, Henry Julian, 1333
Abrams, Charles, 1334
Acheson, Dean, 341-45
Adams, John Clarke, 380
Adams, Richard N. , 646
Adams, Sherman, 279
Adams, Walter, 1592
Adelman, M. A. , 1457
Ader, Emile B. , 179
Adler, Selig, 346
Agar, Herbert, 19, 347
Ahearn, Daniel S. , 1569
Albertson, Dean, 280
Albright, Raymond J. , 1068
Alexander, Robert J. , 647
Allen, Frederick L. , 1903
Allen, George E. , 85
Allen, Richard C. , 972
Allen, Robert S. , 236
Almond, Gabriel A. , 348, 1221
Alperovitz, Gar, 773-74, 860-62, 946
Alsop, Joseph, 349, 1294-95
Alsop, Stewart, 349, 1294-95
Ambrose, Stephen E. , 723
American Assembly, 532, 535, 1611
American Civil Liberties Union, 1335
American Enterprise Association, 1665
American Heritage Magazine,

Editors, 334
American Historical Association, 1
American Political Science Association. Committee on Political Parties, 26
Amrine, Michael, 775
Amuzegar, Jahangir, 1612
Anderson, Dillon, 1169
Anderson, Jack, 1265
Anderson, John Weir, 1336
Anderson, Martin, 1846
Anderson, Oscar E. , 1104
Anderson, Patrick, 86
Andrews, Bert, 1170
Appleman, John A. , 805
Appleton, Sheldon, 351, 536
Aptheker, Herbert, 863
Armstrong, John P. , 352
Arneson, R. Gordon, 1124
Arnold, Thurman, 1171, 1337
Aronson, James, 864
Ashmore, Harry, 1395, 1423
Association of the Bar of the City of New York. Special Committee on the Federal Loyalty-Security Program, 1172
Atwood, Robert Bruce, 149
Auerbach, M. Morton, 1776

Bach, George Leland, 1570
Bailey, Charles W. , 791-92
Bailey, Stephen K. , 113-14
Bailey, Thomas A. , 87, 353-54

Baldwin, David A., 355, 1613
Baldwin, Hanson W., 1044
Baldwin, James, 1396-97
Ballantine, J. W., 847
Ballard, Hoyt B., 1858
Baran, Paul A., 1458-59
Barnet, Richard J., 356-58, 865
Barnett, A. Doak, 537
Barnouw, Erik, 1760
Barth, Alan, 1173-74
Bartholomew, Paul C., 163
Bartlett, Ruhl J., 359
Bartley, Ernest R., 1654
Bartley, Numan V., 180, 1338, 1424
Barzun, Jacques, 1794-95, 1904
Batchelder, Robert C., 776

Bate, Henry Maclear, 538
Bates, Daisy Gatson, 1425
Bates, Marston, 1847
Bator, Francis M., 1460
Bator, Victor, 613
Bauer, Elizabeth Kelley, 1438
Bauer, Raymond A., 1614
Beal, John Robinson, 360, 539
Beaser, Herbert Wilson, 626
Beaufre, André, 686, 1125, 1156
Bechhoefer, Bernhard G., 826
Becker, Harold K., 3
Behrens, Earl, 65
Behrman, Jack N., 1571, 1590
Beichman, Arnold, 827
Bell, Bernard Iddings, 1905
Bell, Coral, 361, 866
Bell, Daniel, 1715, 1777-78, 1848
Bell, Jack, 88

Beloff, Max, 867, 973
Bendix, Reinhard, 1849
Benedict, Murray R., 1435-38
Bennett, John C., 1126
Benson, Ezra T., 1439
Bentley, Elizabeth, 1222
Bentley, Eric, 1175
Benton, William, 1796
Berelson, Bernard, 181, 1754
Berger, Carl, 974
Berger, Morroe, 1339-40
Berle, Adolph A., 1461
Berman, Daniel M., 1341, 1426
Berman, William C., 237, 1342
Bernstein, Barton J., 238-41, 1440-41, 1462, 1514, 1736-38
Bernstein, Irving, 1694, 1739
Bernstein, Marver H., 1593
Bernstein, Victor H., 806
Besterman, Theodore, 828
Bestor, Arthur E., 1797-98
Beugel, Ernst Hans van der, 724
Bickerton, Ian J., 667
Biddle, Francis B., 362, 807, 1343
Biderman, Albert D., 975
Bidwell, Percy Wells, 1463
Billington, Monroe, 1414
Birdsell, Paul, 847
Black, Hugo Lafayette, 164
Blackett, Patrick M. S., 777, 1127-29
Blackman, John L., 1740
Blair, Clay, 1149
Blanchard, Carroll Henry, 4
Blanchard, Robert, 182
Blanshard, Paul, 1835
Blaustein, Albert P., 1427
Block, William J., 1442

Bloomfield, Lincoln P. ,
363, 829-30
Blum, Robert, 540
Blyth, Conrad A. , 1464
Boarman, Patrick M. , 1666
Bogart, Leo, 1415, 1761
Bogue, Donald J. , 1850
Bohlen, Charles E. , 364
Bolling, Richard, 115
Bollinger, Lynn L. , 1466
Bolner, James, 1398
Bontecou, Eleanor, 1176
Boorstin, Daniel J. , 1906
Borklund, Carl W. , 1045
Bosch, William J. , 808
Bouscaren, Anthony T. ,
694, 868
Bowie, Robert R. , 365
Bowles, Chester, 27-29,
366-69, 533, 579
Bozell, L. Brent, 1266
Bradley, David, 778
Bradley, Philip D. , 1667
Brameld, Theodore, 1799
Branyan, Robert L. , 281
Bray, Douglas W. , 1807
Brennan, Donald J. , 831,
1046
Briggs, Ellis, 976
Brinton, Crane, 725
Brock, Clifton, 30
Brodbeck, Arthur J. , 184
Brodie, Bernard, 779,
1130
Brodkin, E. I. , 1615
Bronfenbrenner, Martin,
1465
Brooks, John N. , 1851
Brooks, Philip C. , 242
Broude, Henry W. , 1515
Brown, Allen, 1152
Brown, Brendan Francis,
819
Brown, Delmer M. , 582,
809
Brown, Emily Clark,
1680, 1716

Brown, Harrison, 1852
Brown, John Mason, 183
Brown, Oliver, 165, 1428
Brown, Ralph S. , 1177
Brown, Seyom, 370
Brown, Stuart Gerry, 31
Brown, William A. , 1616
Brown, William Norman,
580
Bruck, H. W. , 491, 1027
Brzezinski, Zbignieuw K. ,
32
Buchan, Alastair, 1157
Buckley, William F. , 282,
1178, 1266, 1779
Budenz, Louis F. , 1223
Bulletin of the Atomic
Scientists, 1131
Bullitt, William C. , 541
Bundy, McGeorge, 342,
801
Bunzel, John H. , 1594
Burdick, Eugene, 184
Burnham, James, 371,
869, 1224-25
Burns, Arthur F. , 1064,
1516-20
Burns, James MacGregor,
33, 89
Burr, Nelson R. , 5
Burrow, James G. , 1818
Bursk, Edward C. , 1521
Busch, Noel F. , 185
Bush, Vannevar, 1047, 1819
Butow, Robert J. C. , 780
Butterfield, Fox, 634
Butters, John Keith, 1466
Buttinger, Joseph, 614
Byrnes, James F. , 372-73,
695

Cabot, John M. , 648
Cagle, Malcolm W. , 977,
1000
Calkins, Fay, 186, 1695
Calleo, David P. , 1158
Calvocoressi, Peter, 810

167

Cameron, Allan W. , 615
Campbell, Alexander, 542
Campbell, Angus, 187-89
Campbell, John C. , 668
Cannon, Mark W. , 1873
Capitanchik, David B. , 374
Caraley, Demetrios, 1048
Caridi, Ronald J. , 34,
  978-79
Carleton, William G. , 375
Carr, Albert H. Z. , 871
Carr, Robert K. , 1179,
  1344-45
Cassady, Ralph, 1595
Castle, Eugene Winston,
  1617
Cater, Douglass, 35, 1522
Caughey, John W. , 1346
Centers, Richard, 1853
Chafee, Zechariah, 1347
Challener, Richard D. ,
  376, 1091
Chamberlain, John, 608
Chamberlain, Neil W. ,
  1596, 1741-42
Chamberlin, Edward H. ,
  1665
Chamberlin, William
  Henry, 377
Chambers, Whittaker,
  1257-58
Chandler, Lester V. , 1467,
  1572
Chang, Hsin-Hai, 543
Chase, Harold W. , 1180
Chase, Richard, 1907
Cheever, Daniel S. , 36,
  378
Chenery, Hollis B. , 681
Cheney, Richard B. , 118
Chevalier, Haakon, 1296
Childs, Marquis, 283, 1522
Ching, Cyrus S. , 1668
Cho, Soon Sung, 980
Christenson, Reo M. , 1443
Churchill, Winston S. , 379
Claque, Ewan, 1669

Clark, John Maurice, 1468
Clark, Joseph S. , 116-17
Clark, Mark Wayne, 696,
  981
Clark, Thomas D. , 1854
Clark, Tom C. , 166, 1348
Clark, Wesley C. , 1655
Clausen, Aage R. , 118
Clay, Gen. Lucius D. ,
  872-73
Clemens, Diane Shaver,
  758
Cleveland, Harlan, 380
Clover, Vernon T. , 1898
Clubb, Oliver E. , 544
Coale, Ansley J. , 1096
Coblenz, Constance G. ,
  484, 941
Coblenz, Gastro, 393
Cochran, Bert, 190, 1049
Cochran, Thomas C. , 1597
Coffey, Joseph I. , 1068
Coffey, Thomas M. , 781
Coffin, Tristram, 243, 381
Cogley, John, 1836
Cohen, Bernard Cecil, 583,
  832, 835
Cohen, Jerome B. , 584
Cohen, Warren I. , 545
Cohn, Roy, 1267
Coit, Margaret L. , 1469
Colbert, Evelyn S. , 585
Cole, Gordon H. , 1670
Coleman, Richard P. , 1880
Collins, Joseph Lawton,
  982
Colm, Gerhard, 1717
Columbia University.
  Bureau of Applied Social
  Research, 1762
Commager, Henry S. , 20,
  1181, 1349
Commission on Freedom of
  the Press, 1350-51,
  1763-64
Compton, Arthur H. , 782
Compton, Karl T. , 783

Fermi, Laura, 1101
Ferrell, Robert H. , 403, 1623
Fertig, Lawrence, 1528
Fiedler, Leslie A. , 1271, 1320, 1910
Field, Harry, 1762
Fine, Benjamin, 1805
Fineberg, Solomon Andhil, 1321
Finer, Herman, 94, 689
Finletter, Thomas K. , 404-406, 1056, 1097
Fisch, Edith L. , 1899
Fischer, Mary L. , 10
Flash, Edward S. , 1718
Fleming, Denna Frank, 885-86
Fleming, R. W. , 1739
Fletcher, Cyril Scott, 1806
Flynn, John T. , 42, 552, 1187-88
Fontaine, André, 887-88
Forrestal, James, 889
Forster, Arnold, 1360
Fortune Magazine. Editors, 1609
Fox, Annette B. , 1159
Fox, William T. , 1159
Foy, Bernard L. , 1529
Fraenkel, Osmond K. , 1361
Frankel, Charles, 1911
Frazier, Edward Franklin, 1401
Freed, Fred, 786
Freeland, Richard M. , 246, 408, 1189
Freeman, Ralph E. , 1473
Friedman, Leon, 167
Friedman, Milton, 1576
Friedmann, Wolfgang Gaston, 728
Friedrich, Carl J. , 1050
Friendly, Henry J. , 43
Frier, David A. , 290
Frye, Richard N. , 683
Fuchs, Lawrence H. , 44

Fulbright, J. William, 409-10, 890
Futrell, Robert Frank, 986

Gabarino, Joseph William, 1672
Gabriel, Ralph H. , 891
Galbraith, John Kenneth, 1474-78, 1530
Gallois, Pierre M. , 411, 1133
Galloway, George B. , 124
Gardner, John W. , 1912
Gardner, Lloyd C. , 412, 892
Gardner, Richard N. , 1577, 1624
Garson, Robert A. , 201
Gates, Robbins L. , 1429
Gati, Charles, 893
Gavin, James M. , 894
Geer, Andrew C. , 987
Gelber, Lionel M. , 729-30
Gellhorn, Walter, 1190-92
Gerhart, Eugene C. , 813
Gerson, Louis L. , 413, 895
Gervasi, Frank Henry, 45
Gillmor, Dan, 1193
Gilpin, Robert, 1134, 1822-23
Ginzberg, Eli, 1807
Giovannitti, Len, 786
Girvetz, Harry K. , 1782
Glazer, Nathan, 1402, 1882-83
Glueck, Sheldon, 814, 1531, 1895
Golay, John F. , 731
Gold, Herbert, 1913
Goldberg, Arthur J. , 1696
Goldberg, Joseph P. , 1673
Goldman, Eric F. , 21, 1914
Goldman, Ralph M. , 192
Goldschmidt, Walter, 532
Goldsmith, Raymond

William, 1479
Goldwater, Barry M. , 46,
414
Gollagher, Elsie, 288
Golzé, Alfred R. , 1657
Goodman, Walter, 1194
Goodrich, Leland M. ,
837-38, 988
Goodwin, Richard N. , 625
Goold-Adams, Richard, 415
Gordenker, Leon, 989
Gorter, Wytze, 1625
Graber, Doris A. , 416-17
Graebner, Norman A. ,
291, 418-19, 896-97
Gravel, Mike, 636
Gray, Horace M. , 1592
Green, Adwin Wigfall, 990
Green, David, 650
Green, Harold P. , 1102,
1308
Greenberg, Daniel S. , 1824
Greenberg, Jack, 1403
Greenberg, Sanford D. , 91
Gregory, Charles O. , 1674
Grew, Joseph C. , 787
Grey, Arthur L. , 1010
Griffith, Ernest Stacey, 125
Griffith, Robert, 1272-73
Grimes, Alan P. , 1362
Grodzins, Morton M. , 1131
Gross, Bertram M. , 247,
1480
Groves, Leslie R. , 1103
Gruenberg, Sidonie M. ,
1900
Gruening, Ernest Henry,
151-52, 626
Grunder, Garel A. , 609
Guest, Robert H. , 1690
Guhin, Michael A. , 420,
553
Gunther, John, 248, 335,
589, 991, 1915
Gurin, Gerald, 189
Gurko, Leo, 1916
Gurtov, Melvin, 627

Gwertzman, Bernard M. ,
439

Haber, William, 1748
Hacker, Andrew, 1481
Hadley, Eleanor M. , 590
Hagen, Everett E. , 1482
Halle, Louis Joseph, 421,
898, 1135
Hallowell, John H. , 1917
Halperin, Morton H. , 992,
1136
Halperin, Samuel, 675
Hambro, Edward, 837
Hamby, Alonzo L. , 249-50
Hammer, Ellen Joy, 628-29
Hammond, Paul Y. , 422,
899, 1057-58, 1081
Handlin, Oscar, 7, 1363
Hansen, Alvin H. , 1532-33
Hansen, William P. , 221
Harbison, Frederick H. ,
1675
Hardin, Charles M. , 1445-
46
Hardt, John Pearce, 900,
1483
Hardman, Jacob B. S. ,
1697
Harley, John Eugene, 839
Harper, Alan D. , 1196
Harriman, W. Averell,
701-702
Harris, Joseph P. , 47
Harris, Louis, 202
Harris, Robert J. , 1364
Harris, Seymour Edwin,
48, 1484, 1534-36, 1578,
1607, 1626
Hart, Albert G. , 1579-81
Hart, Henry C. , 1658-59
Hartley, Fred Allan, 1719
Hartmann, Frederick H. ,
732
Hartmann, Susan M. , 126,
251
Harvard University.

Jackson, Gabriel, 1199
Jackson, Henry M. , 437,
 1063
Jackson, Percival E. , 168
Jackson, Robert H. , 169,
 817-18
Jacobs, Jane, 1862
Jacobstein, Meyer, 1707
Jacoby, Neil H. , 1584
Jaffe, Abram J. , 1749
James, Dorothy Buckton,
 97
James, Estelle Dinerstein,
 1701
James, Ralph C. , 1701
Javits, Jacob K. , 1064
Jensen, Jay W. , 821
Jewell, Malcolm E. , 129,
 438
Johnson, David Gale, 1449
Johnson, Haynes B. , 439
Johnson, Walter, 98, 204
Jones, E. Terrence, 1539
Jones, Howard Mumford,
 1811
Jones, Joseph Marion, 1629
Jones, Mary G. , 1182
Jorstad, Erling, 1839
Jowitt, William Allen
 Jowitt, 1st earl, 1263
Joy, C. Turner, 999
Jungk, Robert, 1105

Kahin, George M. , 631
Kahn, Alfred E. , 1598
Kahn, Gordon, 1234
Kahn, Herman, 1137-38
Kallenbach, Joseph E. , 99
Kalven, Harry, 1301, 1365,
 1404
Kampelman, Max M. , 1235,
 1702
Kane, John J. , 1840
Kaplan, Abraham D. H. ,
 1487, 1540, 1677
Kaplan, Lawrence A. , 1161
Kaplan, Morton A. , 484,

941
Kariel, Henry S. , 1863
Karig, Walter, 1000
Karsh, Bernard, 1744
Kase, Toshikazu, 593
Katona, George, 1488-89
Kaufmann, William W. ,
 1065
Kawai, Kazuo, 789
Kaysen, Carl, 1607
Kecskemeti, Paul, 1066
Keeley, Joseph Charles,
 555
Keenan, Joseph B. , 819
Keezer, Dexter Merriam,
 1490, 1601
Kefauver, Estes, 1896
Kelley, Stanley, 51
Kelly, Alfred H. , 1366
Kemper, Donald J. , 1367
Kempton, Murray, 295,
 1864
Kendall, Willmoore, 1783
Kennan, George F. , 440-
 42, 911-15, 1630
Kennedy, Robert F. , 1703
Kenworthy, E. W. , 634
Kerr, George H. , 556
Kertesz, Stephen Denis, 443
Kerwin, Jerome Gregory,
 1067
Kesselman, Louis Coleridge,
 1720
Key, Vladimir O. , 205-206
Kie-Chiang Oh, John, 1001
Kieffer, John Elmer, 916
Kinevan, Marcos E. , 155
King, Ernest, 790
King, Martin Luther, 1368,
 1405
Kinkead, Eugene, 1002
Kintner, William R. , 960,
 1068
Kipphardt, Heinar, 1302
Kirk, Grayson, 444
Kirk, Russell, 1784
Kirkendall, Richard S. , 9,

174

Lerche, Charles O. , 454, 920
Lerner, Max, 1921
Leuchtenburg, William E. ,
1660
Levin, Arnold, 707
Lewin, Elizabeth, 1221
Lewis, Anthony, 1373
Lewis, Cleona, 1632
Lewis, John Prior, 247
1480, 1633
Lewis, John W. , 631
Lewis, Richard S. , 1111
Lewis, Wilfred, 1586
Lichtblau, John H. , 1604
Lie, Trygve, 842
Lieberman, Elias, 1706
Lieberman, Joseph I. ,
1142
Lieuwen, Edwin, 652
Lifton, Robert J. , 812
Lilienthal, Alfred M. ,
677-79
Lilienthal, David E. ,
1112-13, 1303, 1497,
1634
Lincoln, Charles Eric,
1406, 1841
Lippmann, Walter, 921,
1922
Lipset, Seymour M. ,1849,1867
Litchfield, Edward H. ,
735
Livezey, William E. , 609
Lofgren, Charles A. , 1005
Lokos, Lionel, 1274
Lomax, Joseph E. , 1407
Lomax, Louis E. , 1374
Longaker, Richard P. ,
102, 1375
Lorenz, A. L. , 257
Loth, David, 199, 1228
Love, Kennett, 690
Lowenthal, Leo, 1867
Luard, David E. T. , 922
Lubell, Samuel, 54-55, 211
Luck, Thomas J. , 1723
Lukacs, John A. , 923

Lundberg, Ferdinand, 1901
Lyle, Jack, 1770
Lynd, Staughton, 924
Lynde, Cornelius, 64
Lyons, Gene M. , 1006

McAdams, Alan K. , 1724
MacArthur, Douglas, 595-
97, 602, 1007-1009
McCain, R. Ray, 1376
McCamy, James L. , 455,
719
McCarthy, Eugene J. , 212,
1785
McCarthy, Joseph R. ,
1275-76
McClintock, Robert, 1073
McCloy, John J. , 456
McClure, Arthur F. , 258,
1679
McConnell, Grant, 1450
McCoy, Donald R. , 1377
McCrary, J. C. , 1866
McCune, George M. , 1010
Macdonald, Dwight, 213
MacDougall, Curtis D. , 214
Machlup, Fritz, 1543
MacInnis, Edgar Wardwell,
457, 925
MacIver, Robert, 1237,
1378
McLellan, David S. , 1011
McLuhan, Herbert Marshall,
1758
McNaughton, Frank, 274-75
McNeill, William Hardy,
458, 736, 926
McPhee, William N. , 181
McWilliams, Carey, 1202,
1868
Madariaga, Salvador de,
927, 1143
Madison, Charles A. , 259
Magdoff, Harry, 459, 1635
Mallalieu, William C. , 1636
Mandelbaum, David Good-
man, 1417

Mangone, Gerard J. , 380
Mann, Dean E. , 56
Mansfield, Harvey C. ,
1075
Manson, Frank A. , 977,
1000
Marcuse, Herman, 100,
296
Margold, Stella K. , 703
Markel, Lester, 460
Marshall, Charles B. , 461
Marshall, S. L. A. , 1012-
13
Martin, Edwin M. , 598
Martin, Harold H. , 1023
Martin, James Walter, 324
Martin, John B. , 215,
1430
Martin, Joseph W. , 57
Martin, Ralph G. , 1869
Marvell, Gerald, 130
Marzani, Carl, 928
Maslow, Will, 1725
Mason, Alpheus Thomas,
171
Mason, Edward S. , 1498-
99
Matthews, Donald R. , 131
Matusow, Allen J. , 240,
1451
Matusow, Harvey
Marshall, 1238
May, Ernest R. , 103, 1074
May, Ronald W. , 1265
Mayer, Herbert C. , 1637
Mayer, Martin, 1759
Mayhew, David R. , 58
Mazo, Earl, 59-60
Meade, Edward Grant, 1014
Means, Gardiner C. ,
1500-1501
Mecham, John Lloyd, 653
Meeker, Marchia, 1891
Mehdi, Mohammad T. ,
680
Melby, Ernest O. , 1812
Melby, John F. , 560, 929
Melman, Seymour, 843,

930-31, 1502
Merkl, Peter H. , 737
Merson, Martin, 1277
Metz, Harold W. , 1707
Meyer, Frank F. , 1239,
1786
Meyer, Michael C. , 18
Meyer, Richard, 182
Meyerhoff, H. , 1312
Michelmore, Peter, 1304
Michigan. University.
Survey Research Center,
462
Middleton, Drew, 738, 1164
Mikesell, Raymond F. , 681
Mikolajczyk, Stanislaw, 844
Milbrath, Lester W. , 132
Miller, Byron S. , 1114
Miller, Elizabeth W. , 10
Miller, Herman P. , 1503
Miller, Merle, 1203, 1240
Miller, Warren E. , 189
Miller, William, 1756
Miller, William J. , 298
Miller, William Lee, 299
Millett, John D. , 1544
Milligan, Maurice M. , 61
Millikan, Max F. , 463,
1638
Millis, Harry A. , 1680
Millis, Walter, 845, 889,
1075
Mills, Charles Wright, 464,
1681, 1870-72
Mollenhoff, Clark E. , 1708
Molnar, Thomas Steven,
465
Monroney, Mike, 1204
Monsen, R. Joseph, 1873
Montgomery, John D. ,
633, 1639
Moon, Henry Lee, 1379
Mooney, Booth, 62
Moos, Malcolm, 192
Morgan, H. Wayne, 260
Morgenstern, Oskar, 1144
Morgenthau, Hans J. , 63,
466-72

Morin, Relman, 336
Morison, Elting E. , 795
Morley, Blaine, 182
Morray, Joseph P. , 932
Morris, Joe Alexis, 516
Morris, Richard B. , 22
Morrow, E. Frederic,
300
Morton, Louis, 796
Morton, Walter A. , 1545,
1750
Mosely, Philip E. , 704-
705, 739-40
Moses, Robert, 325
Mowrer, Edgar Ansel,
933
Mowry, George E. , 23
Moynihan, Daniel P. , 1402
Mueller, John E. , 104
Muller, Herbert J. , 216
Mumford, Lewis, 1874,
1923
Murphy, Charles J. V. ,
301-304, 1546-47
Murphy, Henry C. , 1587
Murphy, Robert D. , 473
Murphy, Walter F. , 133,
172
Murray, Thomas E. , 1145
Murrow, Edward R. , 24
Muse, Benjamin, 1431-32
Muther, Jeannette E. ,
847, 849
Myrdal, Gunnar, 1504

Nash, Bradley D. , 64
Nash, Gerald D. , 1605
National Cartoonists
Society, 337
National Review.
Editors, 1178
Nelson, Donald M. , 1548
Nelson, James Cecil, 1549
Neufeld, Maurice F. , 11,
1697
Neumann, William L. , 934
Neustadt, Richard E. ,

105-107, 134, 305-306,
691, 1875
Nevins, Allan, 1278
Newby, Indus A. , 1408
Newman, James R. , 1114
Newman, William J. , 1787
New York Times, 1373
Nicholas, Herbert, 741,
846
Nichols, Jeannette P. ,
1640
Nichols, Lee, 1418
Niebuhr, Reinhold, 307,
935, 1924
Nieburg, Harold L. , 474,
1115, 1826
Nikoloric, Leonard A. ,
1205
Nixon, Richard M. , 308,
475
Noble, G. Bernard, 476
Nogee, Joseph L. , 1116
Norman, John, 1015
North, Robert C. , 561
Northedge, Frederick S. ,
742
Nourse, Edwin G. , 1550,
1726
Novak, Robert, 41
Novogrod, John C. , 630

O'Brian, John Lord, 1206
O'Dea, Thomas F. , 1842
Oliver, Robert T. , 1016
O'Neill, James Milton,
1843
Opie, Redvers, 847, 1616
Oppenheimer, J. Robert,
1146, 1827
Osgood, Robert E. , 477-
78, 1076, 1165
Oxnam, G. Bromley, 1207

Paarlberg, Donald, 1452
Packard, George R. , 599
Packard, Vance, 1876-77
Packer, Herbert L. , 1241,

Redding, John M. (Jack), 217
Reder, Melvin W. , 1507
Reel, Adolf Frank, 823
Rees, Albert E. , 1745, 1751-52
Rees, David, 1020
Reeve, Wilfred Douglas, 1021
Reeves, Thomas C. , 1208
Reichley, James, 65
Reilly, Gerard D. , 1729
Reinhardt, George C. , 1079
Reischauer, Edwin O. , 600
Reissman, Leonard, 1881
Reitzel, William, 484, 941
Richardson, James L. , 1166
Rickover, Hyman G. , 1813
Riddick, Floyd M. , 137-38
Riddle, Donald H. , 139
Ridgeway, Marian E. , 140, 1662
Ridgway, Matthew B. , 1022-23
Riesman, David, 1814, 1882-83, 1926
Rippy, J. Fred, 1644
Rivero, Nicolas, 656
Roberts, Chalmers M. , 942, 1147
Roberts, Henry L. , 14-15, 744, 943
Robinson, James A. , 141, 485
Rogge, Oetje John, 1383
Rogin, Michael P. , 1281
Rogow, Arnold A. , 1080
Roosevelt, James, 1790
Root, Jonathan, 1327
Roper, Elmo, 66
Rorty, James, 1282
Rose, Arnold M. , 67, 1884
Rose, Caroline, 1884
Roseboom, Eugene H. , 218

Rosenau, James N. , 486
Rosenberg, Bernard, 1769
Rosenthal, Alan, 1102
Rosinger, Lawrence K. , 581
Ross, Irwin, 219
Ross, Thomas B. , 722, 1332
Rossiter, Clinton L. , 109, 1791
Rostow, Eugene V. , 487, 1554, 1606
Rostow, Walt W. , 463, 488, 707, 944, 1638
Rourke, Francis E. , 1328
Rouzé, Michel, 1306
Rovere, Richard H. , 312-14, 489, 1024-25, 1283, 1927
Rowan, Carl Thomas, 1410
Roy, Ralph Lord, 1245
Rozek, Edward J. , 763
Rubin, Morris, 1284
Rubin, Morton, 1885
Rubottom, Roy R. , 657
Ruchames, Louis, 1730
Ruetten, Richard T. , 1026, 1377
Russell, James Earl, 1886
Russell, Ruth B. , 849-50
Ruttan, Vernon W. , 1453

Safran, Nadav, 682
Samuel, Howard D. , 113
Samuelson, Paul A. , 1518
Sapin, Burton, 491, 1027
Sapir, Michael, 1508
Saposs, David J. , 1246-47, 1709
Sawyer, Charles, 68, 264
Schaar, John H. , 1209
Schaffer, Alan, 69
Schapsmeier, Edgar L. , 70, 220
Schapsmeier, Frederick H. , 70, 220
Scheele, Henry Z. , 71

Scheer, Robert, 666
Schelling, Thomas C. , 851
Scher, Seymour, 315, 1685
Schick, John R. , 745, 945
Schilling, Jane Metzger, 1741
Schilling, Warner R. , 1081
Schlesinger, Arthur M. , 221, 946-48, 1024-25, 1307, 1792
Schlesinger, James R. , 949
Schmidt, Karl M. , 72, 222
Schneir, Miriam, 1329
Schneir, Walter, 1329
Schoeck, Helmut, 1650
Schoenberger, Walter S. , 797
Schoenbrun, David, 638
Schoff, Leonard Hastings, 1454
Schramm, Wilbur L. , 1770
Schriftgiesser, Karl, 142, 1555-56
Schubert, Glendon A. , 174
Schultz, Theodore William, 1455
Schuman, Frederick L. , 950
Schumpeter, Joseph A. , 1557
Schwartz, Anna J. , 1576
Schwartz, Bernard, 1384
Schwarz, Urs, 1082
Scoble, Harry M. , 143
Scudder, Kenyon J. , 1897
Sebald, William J. , 601
Seidman, Joel Isaac, 16, 1686
Seldes, Gilbert, 1771-72
Seligman, Lester G. , 1731
Service, John S. , 563
Seton-Watson, Hugh, 951-53
Shadegg, Stephen C. , 73
Shalett, Sidney, 1896

Shannon, David A. , 223, 1250
Shannon, W. Wayne, 144
Shannon, William V. , 236, 316
Shaplen, Robert, 612, 639
Shattuck, Frances M. , 231
Shattuck, Henry L. , 1210
Sheehan, Neil, 634-35
Shepley, James R. , 1149
Sherwood, Morgan, 1830
Shields, Currin V. , 1845
Shils, Edward A. , 1211
Shimm, Melvin G. , 1887
Shimony, Annemarie, 835
Shister, Joseph, 1687
Shoemaker, Don, 1433
Shoemaker, Ralph Joseph, 317
Shogan, Robert, 224
Shub, Boris, 954
Shulman, Marshall D. , 955
Siepmann, Charles A. , 1773
Simons, Anne P. , 837-38
Simons, Henry C. , 1558
Singer, Joel David, 1083
Sitkoff, Harvard, 225
Skolnikoff, Eugene B. , 1831
Slater, Jerome, 658
Slessor, Sir John, 852, 1150
Slichter, Sumner Huber, 1559, 1732-33
Smith, A. Merriman, 318, 338
Smith, Alice Kimball, 1832
Smith, Arthur Robert, 74
Smith, Bob (Robert Collins), 1434
Smith, Bruce L. R. , 1084
Smith, Earl E. T. , 659
Smith, Gaddis, 490, 798
Smith, Hedrick, 634
Smith, Jean Edward, 746
Smith, John Malcolm, 110
Smith, Louis, 1085
Smith, Roger, 611

Smithies, Arthur, 1588
Smuts, Robert W. , 1902
Snell, John L. , 764,
956-57
Snowman, Daniel, 799
Snyder, Glenn H. , 1081,
1086
Snyder, Marty, 339
Snyder, Richard C. ,
491, 1027
Sobol, Norman, 1670
Somers, Gerald G. , 1688
Somers, Herman Miles,
75, 1560
Somerville, John
MacPherson, 1251
Sontag, Raymond J. , 765
Soule, George, 1928
Soward, F. H. , 660
Spanier, John W. , 492,
1028-29
Spencer, Robert C. , 1675
Spinrad, William, 1385
Spriggs, Dillard P. , 1604
Stalin, Joseph, 708-709
Stanley, Timothy W. , 1087
Starobin, Joseph R. , 1252
Stassen, Harold E. , 1561
Steel, Ronald, 493
Steele, Archibald T. , 564
Steelman, John R. , 111,
265
Stein, Bruno, 1753
Stein, Harold, 1075, 1088
Stein, Leon, 1670
Steinberg, Alfred, 277,
382
Steinberg, Blema S. , 1030
Stern, Philip M. , 1308,
1589
Sternberg, Fritz, 958
Stettinius, Edward R. , 766
Stevenson, Adlai E. , 226-
30, 494-96, 710
Stewart, Charles D. , 1749
Stewart, Thomas B. , 156
Stikker, Dirk U. , 1167

Stillman, Edmund O. , 497-
98
Stillman, Richard J. , 1421
Stilwell, Joseph W. , 565
Stimson, Henry L. , 800-801
Stine, Oscar Clemen, 1435
Stoessinger, John G. , 711
Stolzenbach, C. Darwin,
900, 1483
Stone, Isidor F. , 959,
1031, 1929
Stouffer, Samuel A. , 1212,
1253, 1386
Straight, Michael, 1285
Strauss, Lewis L. , 1151,
1309
Strausz-Hupe, Robert, 566
Strickland, Donald A. , 1833
Stripling, Robert E. , 1254
Stromberg, Roland N. , 499
Stromer, Marvin E. , 76
Stroud, Gene S. , 17
Strout, Cushing, 1310-11
Sulzberger, Cyrus L. , 500
Summers, Clyde W. , 1687
Sundquist, James L. , 1888
Sung, Yoon Cho, 824
Supreme Command for the
Allied Powers, 602
Sutherland, Arthur E. , 1213
Sutton, Francis X. , 1607
Swados, Harvey, 1930
Swearingen, Roger, 603
Sweezy, Paul M. , 1458
Swomley, John M. , 1089

Taft, Philip, 1689, 1710-11
Talbot, Daniel, 1269
Talese, Gay, 1757
Tate, Merz, 1117
Taylor, George E. , 610
Taylor, George W. , 1746
Taylor, Maxwell D. , 1090
Taylor, Telford, 640, 1214
Teller, Edward, 1118, 1152
Terrill, Ross, 567
Thelen, David P. , 1286

Walters, Robert S. ,
1647
Warburg, James P. , 519-
21, 715, 752, 857, 964
Ward, Barbara, 1648
Warne, Colston E. , 1692
Warner, Geoffrey, 645
Warner, William Lloyd,
1889-91
Warren, Earl, 176
Warth, Robert D. , 716,
965
Waskow, Arthur I. , 1093
Wechsler, James A. , 1218
Wecter, Dixon, 1932
Wedemeyer, Albert C. ,
577
Weems, Minor L. , 966
Weinberg, Nat, 1688
Weinstein, Martin E. , 606
Weintraub, Ruth G. , 1390
Welch, Robert, 1256
Welch, William, 717
Welles, Sumner, 522
West, Patricia S. , 1808
Westerfield, H. Bradford,
523-24
Westin, Alan F. , 80, 177,
1747
Westwood, Andrew F. ,
1649
Wexley, John, 1331
Weyl, Nathaniel, 1219
Wharton, Michael, 1315
Whitaker, Arthur P. ,
663-64
White, David M. , 1769
White, Lawrence J. , 1608
White, Llewellyn, 1763
White, Theodore H. , 233,
753
White, Walter F. , 1391-
92, 1412
White, William S. , 81-83,
147
Whitehill, Walter M. , 790
Whiting, Allen S. , 1039

Whitney, Courtney, 607,
1040
Whitney, Simon N. , 1565
Whyte, William H. , 1609,
1892
Widick, B. J. , 1699
Wiebe, G. D. , 1291
Wiggins, James W. , 1650
Wilbur, Ray Lyman, 162
Wilbur, William H. , 526
Wilcox, Clair, 1393
Wilcox, Francis O. , 858
Wildavsky, Aaron, 1566
Williams, Oliver P. , 234,
1456
Williams, William
Appleman, 527, 665
Willoughby, Charles A. ,
608, 1041
Willoughby, William R. ,
1567
Wills, Garry, 84
Wilson, Francis, 1793
Wilson, Jane, 1111
Wilson, Paul A. , 744
Wilson, Thomas W. , 967,
1316
Winnacker, Rudolph A. ,
771
Wise, David, 722, 1332
Wittenberg, Philip, 1220,
1292
Wittmer, Felix, 772
Wittner, Lawrence, 859
Woetzel, Robert K. , 825
Wolf, Charles, 1651
Wolfe, Arthur C. , 1713
Wolfe, Bertram D. , 718
Wolfenstein, Martha, 1775
Wolfers, Arnold, 968
Wolfson, Theresa, 1596
Wood, Robert C. , 1893
Woodbridge, George, 1652
Woodhouse, Christopher
M. , 754
Woodring, Paul A. , 1817
Woodrow Wilson Foundation,

TITLE INDEX

AFL-CIO: Labor United, 1696
A. F. of L. from the Death of Gompers to the Merger, 1710
AMA: Voice of American Medicine, 1818
Absolute Weapon, 779
Academic Freedom in Our Time, 1237, 1378
Addresses upon the American Road, 49-50, 428-29
Adjusting to Technological Change, 1688
Adlai Stevenson, 215
Adlai Stevenson: A Study in Values, 216
Adlai Stevenson of Illinois, 185
Adlai Stevenson: Patrician among the Politicians, 190
Adlai Stevenson's Public Years, 226
Administration of American Foreign Affairs, 455
Adventure in Education, 1809
Affairs of State, 312
Affluent Society, 1474
Africa's Challenge to America, 533
After 20 Years, 356, 865
After Victory, 934
Age of Happy Problems, 1913
Age of Imperialism, 459, 1635
Age of Keynes, 1496
Age of Suspicion, 1218
Age of Television, 1761
Agenda for Action, 519
Aggressive War an International Crime, 822
Agricultural Commodity Programs, 1435
Agricultural Policy in an Affluent Society, 1453
Agriculture in an Unstable Economy, 1455
Alamagordo Plus Twenty-five Years, 1111
Alaska Statehood, 159
All in One Lifetime, 372
Alliance Policy in the Cold War, 968
Alliance Politics, 691
Alliances and American Foreign Policy, 477
Allied Military Government of Germany, 728
Allied Occupation of Japan, 598